FORGED
IN HIS FIRE

FORGED IN HIS FIRE

Natasha Sloane

XULON ELITE

Xulon Press Elite
555 Winderley Pl, Suite 225
Maitland, FL 32751
407.339.4217
www.xulonpress.com

Unless otherwise indicated, Scripture quotations taken from the English
Standard Version (ESV). Copyright © 2001 by Crossway, a publishing
ministry of Good News Publishers. Used by permission. All rights reserved.

Library of Congress Control Number: 2024-903291

Paperback ISBN-13: 978-1-66289-399-5
Dust Jacket ISBN-13: 978-1-66289-400-8
eBook ISBN-13: 978-1-66289-401-5

This book is dedicated to my two daughters
and to all the readers,
that are being Forged in His Fire,
fighting the good fight and enduring
until we are home.

Acknowledgements:

First, I would like to acknowledge my Heavenly Father, Jesus Christ, and His Holy Spirit. Without Him, nothing would have been possible, so I give Him all the honor, glory and praise in this project. Second, my two precious daughters whom I love so much. You two have inspired me to never quit and to keep fighting the good fight. Writing and publishing a book is not a one-person effort, and I thank God for His divine connection to Dr. Larry Keefauver and Crossway Publishers. I want to thank them for editing the book, and for Dr. Larry walking me through each step of what it was going to take to complete this project. I would also like to acknowledge and thank Xulon Press and Salem Author Services for their joint effort in the completion of this book. Thank you to all the prayer intercessors and everyone who encouraged me through this experience. Lastly, I wanted to thank my mom Elizabeth Reis, who supported me through this entire project, encouraged and prayed for me. I couldn't have completed this book with out you mom. I love you.

Prologue

One year after I was born, my mother dedicated me in a Pentecostal church called Christian Temple. Growing up I attended Bible camps, vacation Bible schools, and learned a lot at Jersey Village Baptist.

Before the age of eight, I encountered Jesus. Of course, I didn't know it was Him at the time, but I would see and hear Him in the wooded area behind my grandparents' house. We would talk, and He would tell me He had great plans for my life and that it wouldn't always be easy. My grandmother would converse with my mom telling her I was always speaking to someone (unseen), and that it was adorable to witness. I would later find out just who that was, as I had not yet learned of who Jesus was.

At the age of eight, in a small Alabama church where my siblings and I would attend during the summer; I came to accept Jesus into my heart. I will never forget I could not stop crying when I heard about how much people persecuted Jesus and how He was crucified. I received Jesus in my heart, and I was baptized that very same night. It still brings me to uncontrollable tears even today when I hear about the pain He took for us and the sacrifice He made.

Soon after I was baptized, I started to have recurring nightmares. In this nightmare, three black shadow men would break in through the back door. I watched them walk up the stairs to my room and they would stand over me. Since the nightmares started, I was never at peace. It felt more real each night. My mom has told me I was always seeing things in my room as a child.

We moved around a lot after growing up and we attended many different churches, many of them were Baptist. Circumstances changed that lead to me leaving home when I was seventeen. When I was eighteen, I started to go to a Methodist church. Then, I became curious about the Catholic church. I took the classes, and was baptized a second time through the Catholic church. I never got into praying to Mary, but when the priest spoke of Jesus, I was filled with a feeling of the Holy Spirit's presence. It seemed no matter where I was, I could feel His presence but always wanted to know Him more. I was still stuck in bondage, and knew I needed Him, but I didn't realize just how lost I was.

An event happened in my life, and I had to leave where I was living. I left the Catholic church and I went on to attend a non-denominational church. Though I loved Jesus and knew Him as my Savior, I just didn't know how to truly pick up my cross and follow Him.

None of the churches I attended taught the reality of being a Christ follower. I was going to have to learn this truth the hard way.

Events happened in my life when I was growing up, causing me to have extremely bad thoughts which led to suicidal thoughts. However, every time I would try to plan how I would do it, I would hear a whisper saying, "Hold on, I have something better for you." I recognized this voice.

So even though there were circumstances allowing the enemy in to have an extremely large foothold and try to strip me of any worth, dignity, and my identity, God was still the one I would run to when I was in trouble. I can truthfully say my entire life, after hearing about Him and being baptized, I did not ever doubt He was real, or that He loved me. I had this supernatural knowing He loved me, could see me, and hear me. I would talk to Him and even though it seemed I didn't get any response, something always drew me to Him.

I was still very much indulging in sin and didn't know how to get out of it. I used to find solace in listening to music praising Him. Casting Crowns' albums helped me to feel close to Him. I used to repeatedly play, "I will praise you in this storm," which would bring me peace. My life was a constant struggle. I couldn't find peace outside of music and I made many bad and wrong choices based on emotion and my hurt.

I later found out from the Lord Himself, those three shadow men were demonic presences assigned to me to cause turmoil, anger, and chaos in my life. They followed me my entire life.

I wanted to give God control, but felt very afraid if I did, things wouldn't work out the way I wanted them to. I found out He was always right. They didn't turn out like I wanted; they worked out better when I gave Him control!

Table of Contents

"Those who live are in the flesh…
live unto themselves, those who are in the Spirit…
live unto Christ.
There are two moral characters that are essentially
different, and this is the radical difference
between them."

– A.W. Tozer, *The Holy Spirit*[1]

---

[1] Goodreads.com

Chapter 1

Sins, Reaping What Was Sown

So I say, live by the Spirit, and you will not gratify the sinful nature. For the sinful nature desires what is contrary to the Spirit, and the Spirit is contrary to the sinful nature. They are in conflict with each other, so that you do not do what you want. But you are led by the Spirit... (Galatians 5:16-17 NIV)

Here I was, divorce papers in my hand and pride in my heart. Feeling justified for leaving, I did not want to admit there was a better way to work out what had been bothering me in our marriage. I let resentment and pain build and covered up my pain with smiles, not to mention the pain from my past. I took the coward's way out. I chose someone else over my husband and my children, too. This led to a bitter, acrimonious, and emotionally draining divorce.

For the first year after the divorce, I had the normal schedule of the girls living with me and their dad coming to visit. Their life was easy going and as normal as it could have been with their parents going through a divorce. I moved in with my mom to help me, so I wasn't alone.

During that year, The Lord gave me many opportunities to look at things His way. He tested my heart, and I failed big time. I was mean, bitter, and arrogant. I thought, this was Texas, moms always win, and I have done nothing worthy of not having my kids. At this time in my life, I loved God and believed He was real. I listened to Christian music and even attended church sometimes. However, I was still fully engaging in sin daily.

I only prayed when I needed something, never when I was doing good or to thank Him. Some developments in the custody case arose and it required me to have the girls full time for a short while until everything got sorted out. I was prideful and believed I was owed my children because they were mine. Finding every fault in my husband to keep my anger alive, I needed to keep my actions justified while always wanting to believe the worse in him.

The choice to make this arrangement permanent, at least until the trial, was given to me. I was consulting with others who had the same anger-driven mind sets I did, speaking in the flesh, and covering up my own sadness about what was happening, I made the choice to tell my attorney to go for it. That week leading up to my time to face the judge, I began to feel different, I felt an overwhelming number of emotions. I felt worried for my husband, even though I would never admit it to anyone, but God knew my heart. I couldn't control myself; I was crying non-stop. I felt in my heart and spirit, I may be making the wrong choice and maybe I didn't know all the facts I saw only what my attorney showed me and only what I wanted to see.

Truism:
When you are upset with someone, no matter what they do right, you will always find fault with them.

The morning of the hearing, I went earlier than everyone. As I was sitting in the hallway waiting to see the judge, I felt a pulling in my spirit almost as if I needed to be somewhere else. I called out to God for help, with a true desire to change. I told God I was willing to go through the hard work to do it.

> *"God, I prayed, if my girls are going to have the best life, I can't stay the same. If I am going to change, I don't know where to start. I am hurt and angry and I need Your help. I don't want to keep living this way. I mean it this time with my full heart to give to You. I am giving You my all and*

3

I am telling You to take over my life and my heart. I can't do this anymore. I am so tired. I won't take the driver seat back this time."

Many times, in the past, I would repent and give Him short-lived moments of control, but it never stayed. This time, though, my spirit was quickened with what felt like a whisper.

"Okay, My daughter, He said. You have been doing things your way for a long time, now it's time to do it My way, but in order to move you forward, I need to take you backwards first. Hold on as it will not be easy, but I will be with you."

I didn't know if it was me talking to myself or not, (the voice did have familiarity to it.) However, I knew I wouldn't have told myself I am going to have to go backwards in order to move forward with my life. Right after hearing from God, everyone was shocked by the court's decision. Both my husbands parents would have more opportunity than me to see our girls. I knew this was God's doing. I knew this was not going to be easy, but I made a promise to myself come hell or highwater, I was going to fight this battle to make the necessary changes in my life all the way to the end.

I still walked around with all the same chains and the same things that kept me in bondage, but I knew I was on my way to freedom. I didn't know how long it would take or what freedom would look like, but I knew it was the fight I was willing to engage in for myself and my family. I started this divorce to prove I was justified in leaving. By this time, I was seeing this fight about custody was proving I couldn't do this alone or my way any longer. If I was going to make it through, I needed someone who had a track record of never failing and was always victorious.

I needed my King, Almighty God as my counselor, guide, and battle commander.

Pause and Reflect

Is there anyone in your life right now God could be using to test you? ____

Are there any situations where you could have acted differently?

Explain:

Are you ready to stop trying to do things your way and set your life on God's path? _____

Pray: *Father, I ask You to forgive me of my unknown and known sins. I plead the blood of Jesus over me and over this situation or my enemy _____ (name. I ask Your Holy Spirit to come into this situation and show me the error of my ways and help me right the wrongs. Help me, Father to bind up the spirit of division and chaos. I declare and decree victory over this situation and I loosen the fruits of the spirit over me and my enemy. Help me to walk with a heart full of love and help me to have eyes to see this situation the way You want me to and may you bring healing and reconciliation to this situation. In Jesus' mighty name, Amen.*

"Kairos is a passing instant when an opening appears which must be driven through with forces if success is to be achieved." – Wikipedia

Chapter 2

A Kairos Moment

I was ready. I was determined. There were days, I would have to ask myself am I fighting for the girls, me, or to continue to justify what I did wrong? Sadly, even as I was asking these questions, I was still seeing the guy I left my husband for. This person was long distance, so it allowed me more time alone to focus on learning about God and trying to understand what it meant when preachers would say, "God told me." I wanted to serve God, but I also wanted what I thought was best for me. It wouldn't be until much later I would discover I held on to this person because I felt I had to.

The replaying thought, "I couldn't have just given everything up for nothing; or had I?"

Thankfully I was chasing after a redeeming God who would take all the days I thought were wasted, restore the time, and give it all back to me. However, deliverance and freedom are a process, not an overnight occurrence.

So, I dove into the Word, but I didn't know where He wanted me to read. I would ask Him to guide my hands to the pages He wanted for me, and I asked Him to speak to me. It never failed. I would open the Bible and there would be a verse or a story coinciding with what I was facing in my life. The words came jumping off the page, and straight into my spirit and convicting me in every area.

I found every sermon I could find on God and about people in the Bible who went through tough times and came out on top. As I matured in spirit, He now tells me where to go or shows me a verse.

As I started out, this was how I read the Bible. "If you are wanting to know where to start in the Bible, I encourage you to read and start with John and Colossians."

I started to attend church, with each sermon, I became more excited to know God. There is a radio station here called KSBJ, and they announced a 30-day challenge with only listening to praise and worship music. Then they wanted to hear how it changed the caller's life.

I started it, however, I wanted more. I wanted to go deeper. So, I went passed thirty days. What happened was nothing short of a miracle. My mood shifted quickly, and I was feeling happier. Anytime, I started to feel angry or fearful, I would put on my praise and worship music. I would literally feel the atmosphere shift.

It was a day-by-day process. I wanted to jump ahead, but I could feel Him slowing me down.

I had a lot of insecurities, and it took me a while to feel secure enough to raise my hands in worship. I recall closing my eyes during praise and worship one Saturday night, and hearing the Holy Spirit say, "Raise your hands." I felt a peace come over me. I raised my hands in worship, closed my eyes, and felt I was alone before Him. I felt so safe and secure even though everything was still crumbling around me. It didn't matter in these moments.

I would go on my visits and always had the best time seeing my girls, even though circumstances around me were not the best. I was slowly learning how to focus on what I did have and not what I didn't. It was hard, though. I would go feeling humiliated, but it didn't stop me. I would cry myself to sleep every night, but that didn't stop me from getting out of bed every morning ready to fight.

God saw this nobody, this one girl among 8 billion people, and loved me. I was struggling with being mean, angry, bitter, stubborn (the one that would take the longest be set free from), vindictiveness, selfishness, entitlement, pridefulness, spiteful, controlling, people pleaser, know it all, weak, the victim, no self-worth, a sharp tongue with words that could tear apart, never could be alone, needed constant validation, always had to have a boyfriend, and worst of all, an adulterer. Even with all of that, He chose to save me.

He chose to walk it out with me until everything was uprooted. He wanted me and I wanted Him. My whole life, I wanted to be loved and accepted. He accepted and loved me just the way I was, broken. I felt invincible knowing He loved me. I knew the challenges ahead were going to be hard and there were going to be days I'd want to quit, but I couldn't. My girls needed and deserved a mom who was willing to fight. As I walked with that motivating me, I started to change into who I needed to become, who God created me to be.

I grew up feeling that even though He could hear me, He was still too busy for someone like me. I would talk to Him, but never would get anything back. I kept seeking and knocking, I was not giving up, I was determined. I had an extremely persistent personality, and I was going to use it to find and get to know Him the way He said we could in His Word. I could feel His love through His Word and through times spent in worship I could feel His presence.

I wanted more, and to go deeper with Him. I started to chase Him relentlessly and He was chasing me. Still, I had chains holding me down. I used every ounce of energy I had to fight through it. I didn't know how to pray, so I'd ask Him to help me. I started to see suggestions pop up on my YouTube.

God answers prayers in many ways.

Then one day, I heard a pastor say God is waiting for us to ask Him for the impossible. His fire for the Lord excited me and gave me my blueprint to start praying.

- I was opened to understanding God is alive and wants to answer prayer.
- I learned He wants us to ask Him to perform miracles for us.
- I learned He wants to reveal Himself to us through His word and through a personal relationship with Him.

As I started to pray more, ask for His help more, and most of all, believe He was hearing me:

- I could feel glimpses of joy in my spirit.
- I started to feel stronger.
- My mind was not racing with as many condemning thoughts.
- I knew when I was angry, I could start to recognize it though I didn't know how to stop it just yet.
- I could start to see things with more clarity.

The Day My Life Changed Forever

Then, the day came that changed my life forever. On this day, the veil was lifted, and I was able to see things with a clearer perception.

A loud almost roaring thunder filled my car. I almost wrecked my car I was trembling and crying with a fear and reverence for what I was hearing and experiencing.

"My daughter, I AM who you think I AM. I have been with you since before you were born. I want to tell you this battle, this fight is JUST for YOU. This is not about anyone else; this isn't even about the girls." He said, "You have started things and feared the success in finishing them because you have a curse over you not allowing things to be finished in your life. I am going to teach you how to finish what you started. This battle will be the most brutal one you will have to endure in your life and it will be long, but it is intended to help develop you into the woman you were always meant to become."

He continued, "I am going to teach you how to walk through the fire and not get burned and all of the pain and suffering you will experience will not be in vain. It will be to help many people."

Then, He began to explain my mission, "I am looking for people like you who have unshakable faith, bold and fearless ones like you who I can use and send out to show My people I am real, I am alive, and I want My children to talk with Me. I will also use you to show the world the enemy is real. The enemy will no longer deceive My people. I want to show My people I can still part the seas and send fire down from heaven. I want to use you as My spokesperson.

"The line in the sand is being drawn, and soon I will no longer allow middle ground. People are either for Me or against Me."

I was crying my eyes out hearing this. He kept on going, though, flooding me with insight into why my life has not been easy and why the hits came at me so hard. He explained I had a strong and specific anointing, and the enemy never wanted me to get to this moment. He told me He would reveal it later when I was ready.

Truism:
God will not give you everything at once.

The enemy had tried many times to destroy me in different ways growing up. The enemy knew who I was before I ever did. He attacks in infancy what he fears in maturity.

After hearing this, I declared out loud, "As of this day, the enemy has stolen all he is going to steal from me. I won't give him anything else of me."

Truism:
The enemy sees your greatness before you do,
so, he tries to destroy you from the moment
you are born.

I was in shock from all He had already told me, yet He continued speaking. He told me as I continued to walk with Him, He promised I would declare victory in His name over the entire situation, not just the present circumstances. He meant the totality of the divorce, and my God-given destiny for me and for my future generations. I would later find out that I was already fighting from the victory through Jesus Christ

I had not yet learned what it meant that the Holy Spirit is the bringer of all truth. At this time, my faith was low and had not been tested. Boldness had not grown in me to cover my fears. I didn't know how to use the word of God as my weapon or know how to pray with authority through Jesus Christ. When God declared this over me, He saw who I was to become and was speaking the future truth over my life. It was just like when He told Joshua, "Look, I have given you the land," even though it was occupied by the enemy. God speaks to us what He already knows will happen.

There were many more things He spoke to me during this initial encounter. As I continued to walk through my journey with Him, we would have many more long conversations. His Spirit was forever connected to mine, and there has not been a day since I have not spoken with the Holy Spirit and felt His encompassing love around me and through me.

People ask me, "Why does He talk to you so much?"

The answer is simple. I am always asking Him questions. I wanted to know Him, and I wanted to hear directly from Him. I was curious and didn't want to miss one day without getting to know my heavenly Father, my Creator, and the One who loved me and chose to save me. I had this loyalty to Him I didn't fully understand until years later.

Even after my promise and declaration to not let the enemy take things from me, I still had many more hits I was going to have to face. I was entering a season where I was going to reap everything I had sown in the past, everyone I hurt, every idle word spoken, and any seed I planted, good or bad. God's laws are final. Therefore, we will never get away from reaping what we sow in this life. It will eventually come back around full circle.

> *Do not be deceived; God is not mocked, for whatever one sows, that will he also reap. For the one who sows to his own flesh will from the flesh reap corruption, but the one who sows to the Spirit will from the Spirit reap eternal life.* (Galatians 6:7-8 ESV)

At the Foot of the Cross

Every trip I would take to my husband's house, I would have to pass a 40-foot white cross. One day, a person riding in my car with me suggested we walk over to it. The wind picked up as we got closer to the cross. Walking around behind it by myself, I heard His Spirit say to mine, "Meet me here tomorrow, My daughter, and come alone." I smiled and nodded.

The next day, I ran to the cross with a journal and drink in my hand. There were seats made from stone around the cross. Behind it were two trees with an opening between them to sit on the grass. I had brought a blanket, and from then on, I would be there sitting at the foot of the cross.

God always blessed me with great jobs which gave me freedom to work from a home office, or out in the field. He set this up for me so I could spend time with Him. This was the time He wanted me to focus on His voice and learn to discern it above all other voices.

He told me, "In the future, I am going to tell you to make some hard moves and make choices many will misunderstand and mock you for, but I will need you to trust I am the one telling you to do these things."

Before I knew it, the guilt of leaving, the pain of missing my daughters, and the overwhelming reality I had so much work to do came flooding in. He told me He would take it one day at a time with me.

The Holy Spirit started to reveal to my spirit where I had been wrong in my life. I wrote each one down and then lifted my hands with my palms up and released them to Him as I repented. No flesh taught me to do this. It was all guidance from His Holy Spirit.

When I chose to listen to my attorney, so-called friends, and people who didn't know fully what was going on gave me advice from their flesh, I would jump ahead of Him. I would do what I thought was best and it would backfire again.

Jesus said, "I am the way, the truth and the life."[2] If we are not willing to face the truth, we can't face Jesus. We need to ask Him to help us face the truth about ourselves so we can obtain ultimate freedom in Him.

There were days I was so stubborn; it would take me hours to get over being angry when He exposed me to myself. I would try to argue I wasn't that bad, and He would wait while I pouted, clenched my jaw, and even threw my Bible a few times. (Not recommended). I was horrible, and yet His unfailing love kept pouring into me. Even though it was hard on me, I didn't want to quit.

I was not always willing to see where I was wrong, but He was willing to wait for me to receive the truth.

I would argue with Him about how the people I was hurt by were wrong, too, and He would tell me, "That may be so, but My daughter, this is not about them, this is about you and where you went wrong and how you could have avoided that situation altogether."

---

[2] See John 14:6

It was a rough several years. Yes, I said years. Don't be as stubborn as me. It was hard and humiliating seeing what I was trapped in.

Truism:
Before God will expose anyone else to you,
He will first expose you to you.
You can't help others get rid of the very thing
trapping you.

Each time I felt set free of a chain, I would go back to our secret place, and He would say, "Now, are you ready to see why you acted and felt that way and get rid of the cause?" Then He would reveal the spirit behind it, and we would go deeper together. Each time we went deeper, each layer was more painful than the last one.

When I was walking through these seasons with Him constantly revealing areas within me, I had to make a mental effort to not quit. I knew I could not make it without asking Him to equip me with the strength and endurance to see it through. He was pleased I was finally asking Him for His help and not relying on man. I kept reading and hungering for His Word and trusting His promise I would make it through the specific events of each season. After I was ready to move on from those areas in my life, that season would end, and I would enter a new season with new challenges and even harder tests. *In 1 Peter 4:12 it says: "Beloved, do not be surprised at the fiery trial when it comes upon you to test you, as though something strange were happening to you."*

There were days when I'd start to feel like a failure and want to give up. His Holy Spirit would come with warmth and love and tell me He loved me, and had a beautiful future planned for me. However, if I wanted to make it, I had to put the weight on Him and I had to keep walking each season out. So, I kept going. I chased Him, I waited for Him. I was being tested and challenged to do it His way and on His timetable. Through it all, He kept telling me and showing me how much He loved me. He would flood my spirit with scriptures that confirmed what He was saying to me. He revealed to me how every time I wanted to do it my way or tried to force something to happen, I would fail.

There are times God will take us through a losing season to reveal we need to let go of the control and let Him have His way.
His way is the best way, and He always has our best interests in mind.

Pause and Reflect

Do you feel you're hitting a roadblock?

Sometimes, God allows every door to shut, and removes jobs, and people from you to show you to rely on Him for everything.

Is there a situation right now you are facing God may be trying to use to humble you and expose an area to you?

Could He be trying to help you face and break a cycle or pattern causing you discord in your life?

Pray: *Father God, please reveal what You are trying to teach and show me that is causing the discord in my life and keeping me bound in a destructive cycle. Please show me where I am still trying to do things on my own instead of relying on You for direction and guidance. I am submitting my will for yours. Thank You, Father, for what You are doing in my life. I love You and want every area of my life to serve and please You.*

Record what the Holy Spirit is revealing to you and what God wants you to face and deal with in your life.

Call Me Dad

> *If you then, who are evil, know how to give good gifts to your children, how much more will your Father who is in heaven give good things to those who ask him!* (Matthew 7:11 ESV)

God became my greatest teacher, guide, and my Dad.

One day at church, I had my hands up and He asked me why I was so angry, I told him I felt I didn't have the love of a real father and I felt rejected by so many people. I was hurting and I knew this was why I always wanted to date older men. I wouldn't admit this to anyone out loud, but I knew I wanted a partner and to feel safe and secure. For some reason, my brain felt if I had an older partner, it would fill the void of not having a father.

After I told Him what I was feeling with tears gushing from my eyes, He came back and said, "My daughter, I have been your Father from day one. I have chased you, loved you, and know you have wanted to hear this your whole life. 'I am proud of you.' I am Abba, I am your Dad so you never again will need to search for a Dad. I am He."

From then on, He was my dad. There were days I would argue with Him like a teenage daughter. He knew what I needed and when I needed it. He was the only one who could stand up to me and break me down from my stubborn heart and destructive ways. He was the only one who never gave up on me.

My study times with Him in our secret place became daddy and daughter dates. After the night He confirmed He was my Father, all I wanted to do was spend time with Him, please Him, and make Him proud. I wanted to shut the world out and just worship Him. Without even realizing it, I was being set free from what others and the world thought about me. All I cared was what He thought of me. He saw me at my worst, and He still gave me His best!

Pray and thank Your heavenly Father for loving and being there for you through every situation in your life.

"It is impossible for any of us to worship God without the impartation of the Holy Spirit."

– A. W. Tozer, *The Holy Spirit*[3]

[3] Goodreads.com

Chapter 3

A Relationship with God

Through this time, even though there were spiritual attacks coming coupled with Him removing things from my life, I couldn't help seeing all He was doing in my life and all the things He was exposing to me about myself.

He was giving me new eyes and He brought me so much meaning and understanding in my life.

For example, unbeknownst to me, the court's attorney brought on her friend of ten years to go against me in court and to say whatever narrative she and the other side wanted. I am not even fully aware if my husband knew about this or not.

After a few visits and being watched by this woman, she started to open up to me about what was bothering her. She shared she had been strategically brought on to ensure a bad report was written about me. She explained how she and the court's attorney used to live together and how they had been friends for over ten years. She took this job for the extra money.

However, after meeting me and seeing me with my girls, she felt taking this case to do what they agreed to do was completely wrong. She saw God's encompassing love flow through me to her and opened up to me about a personal dilemma she had which did not pertain to the courts. We became close friends. She no longer wanted to be a part of helping make me look bad. She wanted to expose the truth.

Later, she voice-recorded their conversations and allowed me to hear how she, the judge, and others had all agreed no matter what good I did or how many good reports about me as a mother came in, they were not going to allow me to have any relief, or any requests granted. God exposed the injustice, but He still wanted me to walk through it.

Now, I knew what I was up against. I knew I was not fighting against flesh and blood, and I was going to have to fight this another way. I would still need to walk it out in the flesh, but I was going to have to fight this in prayer. It was easier said than done, though. I would get angry and upset about how this was continuing for so long.

I would run to my Heavenly Father crying and asking why, and He would gently speak to me and tell me, "Your pain has a purpose, My daughter. Trust Me, know I love you, and I am proud of you. If you need strength, ask Me. If you need peace, ask me and I will give it to you. However, this is much bigger than you could ever imagine. This is not just about you, this about everyone attached to you."

I would find out later exactly what He meant. If I had written my story a few years ago, I would have focused on all that happened during my custody battle. However, as I look back on those days, I can see there were many things going on in the flesh that didn't compare to what was going on with me in the spirit.

At the same time my custody battle was dragging on, I was getting stronger. I could meet someone and see what spirits were on them, and I could see demonic attachments. I could see if witchcraft was being used on them. I would know what they had gone through and could even tell them things they prayed for in their most private sessions with the Lord.

I was also flooded with visions on a daily basis. I would know things coming up ahead of time and watch them come to pass. I had visions and many dreams, and I would somehow know what they meant. As I grew closer to His Holy Spirit, I found He was giving me discernment, knowledge, and wisdom to allow others to see it was Him who was talking through me.

I would hear His Holy Spirit speak to me, and tell me, "Go tell them this."

As I obeyed and walked up to them, I was given deeper things and exact words to say only His Spirit knew. He would confirm each message with His written word. He used this information to prove I was sent by God to give them this message.

I started to yearn for my prayer time with Him and crave His word. I would pray and unexplainable things would happen. When I prayed, it felt like I left where I was, and I was transported to another place. I could see fire coming from my hands when I was praying. I experienced many beautiful visions. Sometimes, I left earth and was brought to heaven. It was unreal to experience the beauty, the peace, and the love all around me in heaven. I didn't want leave there.

As I progressed, I knew I was ready for my next steps. I knew I was entering another season once again.

Graduation

I was at church and closed my eyes for prayer. I saw myself in a blue graduation gown and a blue and gold graduation cap. I went to the cross that evening to find out from my Father what this all meant.

I stood at the cross and I heard Him say, "Tonight, My daughter, you are graduating, and I am promoting and elevating you in the spirit. I am going to show you through My Word, and later this week, I am going to walk you through why you know things about people's lives, why you know the things you do, why you have visions and dreams, and how I will always give you My Word to confirm it. I am going to teach you how to test everything you get to ensure it is from Me. I AM not the author of confusion."

Through this season, in our secret place, I would hear Him speak about chapters in the Bible. His Holy Spirit would take me to many different books in the Bible. He would tell me to read them, meditate on them and talk with Him about it when I was done. I would read, write down my thoughts in my journal, and wait for Him to speak.

Truism:
Most people who pray believe it is just them speaking to God, but one of the most beautiful things about prayer and what transitions it from just a one-sided request or even a ritualistic feeling, is when we sit there and wait for Him to speak to us.

Wait for Him to guide you.
Listen for His Holy Spirit to speak to you.

Pause and Reflect

> *How many times have you rushed through prayer and made it about you, and not Him?*

Put the book down right now and take a while to sit in His presence. If you have to put some music on to help you, that's great, but I want you to just sit, and not ask Him for anything. Thank Him and wait for Him.

The Journey

Everyone's journey is different. Some may have had mentors and teachers. Some may have started out to prove the existence of God is false, and some have left the new age culture in search of His truth. Whatever your journey is, it's yours.

Mine, was God's Holy Spirit as my teacher, and it became my most epic and greatest love story. He was the One who disciplined me, gently corrected me and the only One who could understand my complex ways. He never gave up on me.

No matter what your journey looks like, the main things that will lead to a life of freedom are:

- ➢ Developing your faith in Him.
- ➢ Making Him a priority in your everyday life.
- ➢ Allowing Him to reveal the hard truths about yourself.
- ➢ Trading your own desires for the desires He has for you.

> ➢ Going to Him in every decision, praying, waiting for the answer, then obeying Him, and trusting in His love.
>
> ➢ Taking everything, you receive back to His word.
>
> ➢ Take every day He gives you and consistently carve out a special time to spend with Him.
>
> ➢ Ask Him to help you keep a heart willing to repent and forgive.
>
> ➢ Ask Him to give you eyes to see people the way He does.
>
> ➢ Ask Him to become your teacher.
>
> ➢ Remember, a life without time with Him will leave your spiritual armor unpolished and allow chinks in it that will cause you to stumble.
>
> ➢ Jesus said man cannot live on bread alone. The Bible is God's written and spoken word. It is a map for you. Read and meditate on it daily.

Jesus told His disciples the Holy Spirit would bring all truth to them. Without your alone time with the Holy Spirit, He will not be able to reveal to you all the mysteries and hidden secrets of the Kingdom of God and give you divine strategy on how to fulfill God's purpose He created you for. Hearing God's voice is a birthright to every believer.

There is a discipline we need to have when we are working on our relationship with our Father and savior.

Spending alone time with Him in my secret place, allowed Him to show me many things. For example: He would reveal to me when an enemy was coming against me or trying to set a trap for me, (key word trying), speaking word curses over me, or trying to harm me. He would reveal it then show me the blueprint of how I was **not** going to have to fall in the snake pit, but walk around it.

He revealed how He was going to use me on this earth and how everything has a divine purpose in my life and the life of the others I am called to help. He showed me things coming to our country and the body of Christ that were astonishing to see.

There is nothing more exciting than when the Creator of the universe tells you He made you for a specific purpose and then reveals some of it to you.

> *Wouldn't it be nice if you could know when an attack was coming against you, and He showed you a way to avoid it all together?*
>
> *How would you like hearing His Spirit say to you, "This is what is coming, you don't want to do that?"*

He showed me angelic fights and what happens when I pray with the authority given to me through Jesus Christ. It was in my alone time with Him where

He told me, "My daughter, stop saying please. I gave you authority and dominion through Jesus Christ. Here's how you pray to move mountains. I am waiting for my people to ask, command, declare, and believe Me to do the impossible."

If you feel stagnant in your prayer life, pray this the way He showed me for yourself:

> *Father, in Jesus' name, I command through Jesus Christ You to move this mountain before me (insert name of the mountain _____). I declare through the authority You have given me it shall be done as Your Word has promised. I believe You will do the impossible in my life just as You promised in Your Word. Thank You, Father this situation is already resolved.*

Target Prayer

He taught me what I call target prayer. I was to listen to His Holy Spirit to guide my prayers for what He wanted and needed me to pray for through my prayer. He guided me how to remove my flesh out of the way and allow Him to lead. I asked Him to talk me through everything. I wanted to learn to discern His voice. I wanted to do it right. I would ask Him what He wanted me to wear. When a text would come in, I would ask Him how to answer it. Full disclosure, my wants got in the way of His voice many times. He had a remedy for that which was failure.

Failure can be the greatest gift. It allows us to see what not to do and allows us to see we can't and won't ever be able to do this life on our own.

I asked questions every day. I even asked Him His favorite color. I had a thousand "whys." I would ask, then I would pause and listen. Most of the time, He would answer me and when He would respond, I would write down everything He was saying to me. I thought it was the most wonderful thing. The God of the universe talking to me. He gave me understanding, He disciplined me, He made me smile when I felt there was nothing to be happy about and He quickly convicted me when I was in the wrong. He never spoke what I wanted to hear, He spoke what I needed to hear.

He walked with me one day at a time. When I was sad, He would comfort me. When I was confused, He gave me clarity. When I was angry, He would talk me off the ledge of doing (or saying) something towards the person that I would have ended up regretting. The words He spoke I could always find them in the Bible. His voice never changed and will never change. He would never contradict His word and He never will.

One of the way's He taught me how to cause His voice to become louder was my intent.

I learned to ask myself, did I want to hear Him for selfish gain or to be a better person and to learn how to walk an obedient life of serving Him?

Have you asked over and over to hear Him, or for some type of sign? Take a minute to reexamine why you are asking. Is it to benefit you, or is it to humbly bring glory to Him?

Many times, we don't realize we stand in our own way of hearing His voice. We are listening to many other voices.

Ask Yourself…

Am I 100 percent willing to shut out all the noise and to pause everything in my busy life to listen for Him?

Am I willing to shut off the TV, phone, or computer to sit in His presence and listen for what He has to say?

Am I willing to take everything back to His word to confirm it is Him?

Am I willing to present myself a living sacrifice to the Lord Jesus?

Am I willing to submit my will for His?

Through each lesson, the one question, I was asked by Him was "How is your heart postured?"

I had to make a daily and sometimes hourly decision and I had to put in the effort to readdress where my heart was and ask Him how He wanted me to respond to the situations in my life.

I got it wrong many times. He would tell me something, and I would question it, or it would not line up with what I wanted so I would go against Him and selfishly choose for myself again.

He would bring me back to His presence and patiently explained to me, "Until you fully let go, and surrender to what I have for you and let ME lead you, you will continue to walk around the same mountain. My daughter, I will walk with you as many times as you need. I have plans to prosper you."

Assignments for the Kingdom

He encouraged me through every mistake. I would keep asking forgiveness for the same thing and He stopped me one day and His spirit spoke to me "My daughter you have already asked me for forgiveness on this mistake, have you not?" I said "yes", and His Spirit spoke "I have blotted it out, move forward you have bigger things to focus on." Eventually I reached the season where even though to others close to me, it didn't look like I was changing, I knew I was. I was starting to surrender more each day. He would ask me to do something small, and I would listen. The more I would listen, the more He would ask of me.

He told me, "I must be able to trust you with a little before I can trust you with a lot."

One way His voice becomes louder and clearer, is when He tells you to do something, and you listen and then do it. Delayed obedience is still disobedience. As I was starting to do things His way, He started to give me what He called, "Assignments for the Kingdom." They started small such as paying for someone's groceries, or walking in the mall and stopping someone just to tell them God loved them.

I remember being at church and during worship, He shone a light over someone and told me, "Go to them and I will tell you what to say when you get there." I would fearfully go, and before I knew it, He would speak through me and I would see these people coming to tears, falling to their knees, or even grabbing and hugging me tight. I would walk away most of the time not remembering what I said, but knowing His Spirit was speaking through me.

I won't forget when I told this one man, God told me to come and lay hands on his shoulders and pray for his father and a softened heart for the man I was touching. He was hesitant, but I kept eye contact and he knew I was serious. I started to pray, I saw this man, in a wheelchair, I heard His Spirit say, "The man will be healed, that wreck won't steal his legs from him." The man, looked at me in disbelief, crying. After the prayer, he told me his dad had just gotten into an extremely bad wreck and the doctor told him he would be paralyzed for life. I remember seeing the man, walking, I remember each vision I saw, and how The Holy Spirit guided my prayer as I continued to listen. The man was in complete shock when I got done praying what the Holy Spirit was guiding me to say.

God would send me to more people, random people, even people in power and influence. The Holy Spirit knows everyone's heart and needs. He searches everything even the depths of God.

A man needed to hear from God. He was seeking Him. Had I not listened to the Holy Spirit when He told me to go to Him, who knows what would have happened. Because the Holy Spirit sent me to this stranger whom I never met, gave me divine insight to know things he was struggling with he was able to experience the true love of Jesus. As I moved in obedience to the Holy Spirit, I thought, this could be the moment in his life he gave Jesus his full heart. It could be the sign he was desperately hoping for. Whatever it was, the Holy Spirit needed the message to be given to him.

There is a purpose for everything God asks us to do.

Ask Yourself...

Am I willing to walk through things that don't make sense to me?

Am I willing to slow down and wait for Him to lead me?

Will I stop letting fear stand in the way?

Is there something that has been on my mind, or heart I need to do?

Is there a name of a friend or family member that pops up as I was reading this question?

Reach out to them. Listen to the still small voice and do what He is asking. Record in your journal what happens when you do obey His voice.

As you can see, the Holy Spirit is more than my guide, He is my everything. My relationship status went from complicated to serious to madly in love.

At that point, I couldn't live one day without Him. I could see why my life was in chaos before I chose to surrender to Him, do things His way, and give Him my whole heart. The key to stepping into a relationship like this with the Holy Spirit is consistency.

Do you have a very special friend you can count on and love to spend time with?

Wouldn't a relationship with the Holy Spirit be even more special?

Are you ready to give your heart to Him so you can have this exciting relationship with Him as well?

No matter how many times I messed up, He waited for me, He guided me, and He continued to use me. Even when I was feeling ashamed of yet another mistake I made, He waited for me. He searched me out even when I tried to hide from Him. Yes, I was still broken, still in chains, but each day, I felt a little more set free.

Does this sound like you?

Be encouraged because what He has done for me, He will do for you. He wants to!

The more people I helped, the more I became excited and started to seek out assignments and asking my dad for more.

It became more about helping others, then worrying about my problems. My problems were big to me at the time, but God is so much bigger and the people He chose for me to help mattered more.

Here is a prayer you can pray asking God to use you and to give you more so you can help with the increase of the kingdom.

Father, please forgive me for all my sins.

I ask You to use me. I want to be a light in the darkness.

I want to go deeper with You. Will you take me deeper?

I ask for more ability to have discipline, boldness, seek Your wisdom, receive Your visions and guidance for me.

When You know I am ready, send assignments for me to spread the gospel.

Don't let me get ahead of you.

I want people to know You and come into a relationship with You.

Guide my steps Lord and give me the words to speak to reveal Your truth and whatever these people need to be set free.

May Your spirit increase in me and may my flesh decrease.

Use me as Your vessel.

In Jesus name, Amen.

"Solitude with God repairs the damage done
by the fret and noise and clammer of the world."

– Oswald Chambers

Chapter 4

Solitude with God

I was constantly asking for more. Not material things, as you will learn in the coming pages, as He took all material things away from me more than once to test me. He taught me to be content with nothing. Jesus Christ, Father God and the Holy Spirit were my treasure and my reward. I wanted more spiritual wisdom, knowledge and maturity. I wanted to help others. I wanted to share what He was doing, and I wanted others to know He was real. He has an incredible personality, and He loves us so much.

Every day, He had me examining my heart. Even in my anger and bondage, I wanted to please Him. I didn't know how to get rid of my anger and bondage just yet, though. It was a work in progress. I knew each time I was sent to someone, He was using me as a chosen vessel, specifically picked to help them see the heart He has for His people. Seeing people's shock, peace, happiness, prayers answered, and just pure hope and joy led me to see His love and heart for the world.

With each person I encountered, my anger went down. I realized this was so much bigger than me. He was slowly removing all the things keeping me bound. Don't ever let anyone tell you, God can't use you. Even in bondage, God can do the impossible.

Two other short examples of God's wonders and how He can use you even when you are not complete.

I met a man and woman in the courthouse. We were in different courts. While I was in my hearing, I kept getting "go find her" from Him. When I left the court room, I saw the woman about to get on the elevator and I told her I needed to tell her something. I didn't know what it was, but when I got up to her, I saw a vision of a little boy in a large gust of spiraling wind, picking him up and not slowing down. I told her, "I see a young boy, 7-8 and he is stuck in the middle of a huge windstorm. If you do not go and get him from wherever he is now, you will not see him for at least two years and the battle will be long and hard." She received the message from the Holy Spirit. That night, she flew to the state her young son was in. She picked him up at the airport that he was stuck at and brought him home.

About a week later, she called me to let me know she found out someone was planning on taking the boy away and it would have been almost impossible to find him if this happened, and the laws in this other state would have allowed the other side to keep the boy and the fight would have been long. The Holy Spirit gave this woman a warning and because she listened and obeyed, she was able to save her son and herself from a storm God did not intend for her to go through. Not only was I obedient, but the other person received the message from the Holy Spirit, too.

There is a likely possibility at times, that some individuals may not be ready or willing to receive the message. When we give a message from the Holy Spirit to people, it is not our responsibility to worry about how they receive it. Paul says in 1 Corinthians 3:6-11, we are to plant, and we can even water it, nevertheless it is up to God to grow it. We are to give the message and move on, unless the Holy Spirit wants us to also water it. However, it is not our responsibility to ensure they receive it. That is a job for Almighty God Himself.

When you walk with the Holy Spirit, and you encounter other believers who are baptized in the Holy Spirit, they can recognize when the Holy Spirit is speaking, even if He is using a vessel in the flesh.

One of my favorites examples of where obedience was crucial and rewarding for all involved:

I watched "God's Not Dead," for the first time, and at the end of the movie, the Newsboys came on.

I heard the Holy Spirit say, "You will meet with them and pray with them."

I thought, "Okay, now I am letting my flesh get a little too excited to think that could happen."

One month later, I was at a Newsboy's concert. God had miraculously gotten me backstage with someone I used to know, and we both went to line up to meet the Newsboys backstage.

I was one of the first ones in line. I was so excited and then I heard Him say, "Get to the end of the line." I remember thinking, "Ugh, why?" But I went to the back, and I waited until He told me I could go. Anytime someone would come behind me, He made me give them my spot.

My flesh was so uncomfortable, but I kept trusting it was Him talking to me.

I was finally the last person and then a young man came pushing another young man in a wheelchair. The Holy Spirit spoke, "This is why I wanted you in the back. I want you to pray for him and ask the Newsboys to join you. I want you to lead in prayer, and they will accept and join in."

That is exactly what happened, the Newsboys didn't have anyone else behind us, and did not hesitate to join and allow me to lead. Since we were the last ones, the Newsboys were able to take their time with us. They stood in agreement with me through the powerful, healing prayers over this young man who was in a wheelchair. This man was told by doctors from the age of seven, that he would never walk again!

There will be times God will ask us to do things we do not understand, and just like the verse that states,

"You do not understand what I am doing now but one day you will,[4]" rings true. Had I stayed in the front of the line, I would have missed many opportunities.

Getting to lead prayer with the Newsboys was humbling, praying for healing over this young man was even more significant. I was given another opportunity to show God He can trust and use me. I was able to walk out my "Yes" to Him. What was most important to me at this time, though, was showing this person God's love.

Six months later, I saw this young man, who could not walk, walking on a treadmill on Facebook. I cried my eyes out and could not believe what I was seeing. God was healing him, his walk was not perfect, but he was up and out of his chair. That was all the Holy Spirit. That entire night was ordained to bring Him glory.

I started these assignments in 2017, I am writing this book in 2023. There were thousands of assignments He sent me on between those years. I want to be clear, though, I was doubtful, I was fearful, but I asked Him to help me. I felt useless, I felt everything else around me was crumbling, I couldn't keep any healthy relationships, I was insecure, I was lost, but He found me.

When I thought, "How can You use me?" He said, "Let Me show you."

---

[4] See John 13:7

He used me even in my completely broken condition is one of the miracles I will always hold on to. When many people, including my family, couldn't stand to be around me and misunderstood me, He allowed me to be His love to strangers.

> *By grace you have been saved through faith; and that is not of yourselves, it is a gift from God. Salvation is not a reward for the good things we have done, so none of us can boast about it.* (Ephesians 2:8-9 NLT)

Ask Yourself…

> *Am I getting excited to give Him my "yes" yet?*

With each day, week, month and year that passed, I continued to listen to what He told me to do, no matter how crazy it sounded. There will be things the Holy Spirit will tell you to do, no one understands, but this is why getting to know Him, His Holy Spirit, and His voice is so crucial.

God will never ask us to do something to harm anyone. We are to test the spirits of people and what we hear. The Holy Spirit will verify anything He asks of us through scripture. Now, when we ask Him what color to wear, He may not give us a scripture, but when He asks us to be His voice, His hands, and His feet, He will back it up with His Word. We don't need to meditate on what to say either, He will speak through you at the appointed time.

I began to see more and experience more. I started to see spirits around people. Before I even had a chance to ask what spirit it was, the Holy Spirit would provide me with knowledge. I could just look at an individual, and immediately see/know what their bondage consisted of. This did not happen overnight. It happened with a daily desire to have intimacy with the Father, Jesus and the Holy Spirit, along with a postured heart to do it all for His glory and not my own. I did not ask Him for gifts, I asked Him for wisdom and to draw me closer to Him.

Intimacy means to deeply know someone. When we meet someone we want to be with or a new potential friend, we have to make an effort to get to know the person. We have to spend time with them, try different hobbies together, talk with each other, and go through experiences together. That is the same thing we can do with the Holy Spirit.

I was able to obtain intimacy with Him because I wanted to know Him. I wanted to please Him, and I wanted to serve Him. I didn't care what it cost. I just wanted to be with Him.

I have had many people ask me how you get to know Him.

1. Seek to know about Him through God's written Word. His Word is the same yesterday as it is today and will be tomorrow. The more you read His Word, the more you learn about God's nature, His Heart, and His desires for His children.

2. Every day ask Him to give you godly desires and help you walk down paths of righteousness.

3. Change your music selection. Praise and worship can change the atmosphere very quickly.

4. Find a good Bible teaching church.

5. Even if you are afraid, put your hands up in and worship Him with your whole heart.

6. Ask Him what He wants, and not what the world wants you to do.

7. Talk to Him, know He hears you. Even if you don't get an answer right away, keep talking, keep asking, and seeking. He promises those who seek Him with their whole heart shall find Him and those who knock, the door will be open to them.

8. Enjoy your time with Him. You will find He is gentle, He feels, He comforts, He is patient, He teaches and most of all He is just, and He loves His children.

9. Buy a journal, then journal the verses as they minister to you. Record your thoughts, fears, and even start to write letters to Him. Whatever you do, don't stop pursuing Him.

10. If you don't like to read or find yourself getting tired when you pick up the Bible, download a Bible app and listen to the word.

11. Give Him your morning, afternoon, and evening.

    How do you do that you ask, with all of life's demands, work, children, marriage, and more? Make your day about Him.

12. Ask Him to guide your steps. Ask Him to talk with you and tell you clearly if you're not supposed to do something. Ask Him to convict your spirit with what is right and holy. Ask Him to tell you what you are supposed to do. When you hear His soft still voice, listen to it.

13. Re-evaluate your circle of friends. Do the people you hang out with encourage your walk with God or do they seem to hinder, mock it, or try to pull you away from God?

14. Ask Him to help you desire His word, desire His presence and to submit your thoughts under the submission, subjection and Lordship of Jesus Christ.

15. Pray, even if you don't know how, bow your head, and ask God for help. Even if all you have are tears, God hears your heart.

Give Him your time, find a place you love, or find a peaceful place and go there. Just like any other relationship you have it is important to give Him your time. I couldn't have learned all I did without carving out one-on-one time with Him and sticking with it. I would read His Word, write Him poems, write down scriptures, pray scriptures over me, sing and praise Him, listen to praise and worship music, and sometimes I would dance for Him alone under the sky just to worship and thank Him. I would pray every day sometimes for hours, crying out to Him for what He wanted me to pray for and for Him to make me more like Jesus and less like me.

> **The most important thing He taught me was. if I was going to have accuracy, it came from taking my time to sit in silence so I could hear Him and what He wanted to reveal to me.**

I had to shut out the world and other distractions so I could hear Him clearly. He had to come before everyone and everything else. He had to become my number one priority.

Pause and Reflect

Relationships are hard, they are work as many people say. A relationship with the Holy Spirit is work and requires a desire to want to be with Him. The work is not Him, it's within yourself. Allowing yourself to be completely naked and vulnerable without hesitation giving all of yourself to Him for Him to do a new work in you. Facing the raw truth of who you were without Him, facing all the people you hurt, and how you have hurt yourself. Facing the fact you are going to have to forgive people who hurt you, but more importantly, learn to forgive yourself.

This daily alone time was also preparation for what was coming around the corner. The assignment season where He tested not only my faith but my obedience on a level no one would have understood but Him.

Is there a place where you can think of that can be yours and His special place?

Take a minute and close your eyes, what brings you peace, where do you go to clear your head?

Allow His Holy Spirit right now, to show you where He wants to meet you. Write down what He is showing you. Don't doubt the thought or the snapshot of the place He just placed in your mind.

In Joel, it says He will pour out His Spirit on His people and sons and daughters will prophesy, and old men will dream dreams.

In Acts, it says when the Holy Spirit comes on you, you will receive power.

Pray: *Father God, in Your mighty name, I ask for complete forgiveness for all sins, known and unknown. I ask for your grace today. May your Holy Spirit fire be ignited in me. I believe and receive the baptism of Your Holy Spirit. Thank You for equipping me to fulfill the assignments You have for me. My desire is to serve You.*

Being baptized by water is different than being baptized by the Holy Spirit. In John, water is a public display you choose to have Jesus as your personal savior. Being baptized by the Holy Spirit fills you with the power and wisdom to fulfill your destiny.

Note: Throughout my journey to walking in His freedom, I made many mistakes along the way, many! He used each mistake to better my understanding and to help me become stronger. If you were one of the people God used to help show me a mistake, I pray you forgive me and accept my apology and receive my thank you. Your being in my life, helped me be a better soldier for Christ and I can teach others because of what we went through. I can help others to steer clear of making the same mistakes. I have struggled over and over with the same strongholds and behaviors. Sometimes, I would feel as though I took two steps forward and five steps back, but it didn't stop me. He was making a warrior out of me. He told me it would not be easy, but He kept reminding me of the joy that would come with completion in Jesus Christ.

Even if feels hard, the amount of joy coming your way is worth whatever you are facing right now, no matter how hard.

"To fall in love with God is the greatest romance;
to seek Him the greatest adventure;
to find Him, the greatest human achievement."

– Saint Augustine[5]

---

[5] Azquotes.com

Chapter 5

Visions and Dreams

One of the lessons He taught me I want to teach everyone is concerning visions and dreams. He gives His people visions and visions of the night. Some will be figurative, and some will be literal. I would get a lot of visions, but I am going to focus on the ones of people dying as an example. While some were literal, the majority of the ones He gave me were representing dying to their old self, something major in their life was being removed, or something needed to be brought back to life.

I saw visions of people in the hospital, but I learned before I went right out and told anyone what I saw, I needed to ask Him to show me in scripture what He is trying to show me in the vision. I stopped to ask Him:

Does the hospital represent a real place, a spiritual place, or a state of mind this person is in?

Is it really the person He is showing me or does the person represent someone in my life or even a part of myself that needs to go?

*Could the hospital mean this person is
under spiritual attack?*

The only way we will be able to get an accurate interpretation is to take it to the Lord, His word and His Holy Spirit will reveal what the vision means and what we need to pray for this person.

Read and write out these warnings from scripture:

Proverbs 3:7
Romans 12:16

Some visions and dreams can feel very real. I remember I kept getting the same vision for years of this accident on Beltway 8 in Houston. I saw the person in a truck. I saw him choking and coughing and then I saw his hand on the wheel turn straight into an eighteen-wheeler causing a severe accident.

After the very first time seeing this, I felt the pain of losing this person. I had been so angry with this person; God allowed me to feel the pain of losing this person to soften my heart towards him and to pray for him. From that day on, I never stopped praying for him…my husband.

However, when I first saw this vision and felt the pain, I took off and drove around the belt way for hours looking for the exact sign, looking for everything I saw in my vision. It wouldn't be until years later; I learned the wreck I saw was an event that took place in his life literally destroying him. The death and the blood I saw in the vision was how much pain he was in and how without anyone physically seeing it, he died inside that day. It was the day I left my husband for someone else.

In this vision, I saw me running towards the truck and I saw me holding him in my arms crying. He was bleeding nonstop, and the blue shirt I was wearing was being drenched with his blood. It took me years to find out the meaning of this vision.

He was choking while his hand turned the wheel, hitting the eighteen-wheeler. This was a representation of him and his choices that partnered with my choices, and led to me having to see the death it caused in our life.

Later, I saw a vision of him in a coma. I would see after seven years was up, he was new and alive. I came to find out later what the Beltway 8 stood for. In Houston, there is a road that is literally a big circle and if someone gets lost on the road, all they have to do is stay on it, and it would eventually lead them back to the place where they started. I called it the circle road.

I had not yet seen nor learned exactly what caused the wreck in that person's life, and the reason why I was there to observe it. I came to find out the coma meant that even though his body was breathing, inside he was dead. The seven years of him in the coma stood for the seven years it took for God and His Holy Spirit to work

His transformation in me. He gave me a new spirit and a heart of flesh and removed the heart of stone so I could be ready to walk with this person through to his salvation. It was the years I would be required to pray for his salvation so one day he would wake up and be set free.

This is one vision of thousands He has given me, but this one is one that kept repeating itself for years and each year, the vision had more detail than the last. If God is showing you a dream or a vision over and over, there is a message He is trying to get you to notice. His Holy Spirit showed me this person was dead inside and would be until I was complete in Him because He was using my vessel for this person's salvation.

Did you know there are thousands of people attached to your destiny, and nothing occurs by happenstance?

Everything is being orchestrated to fit His grand design and you are part of that design! Someone could be put in your life so you can be the one to help secure their salvation. Even our enemies are in our life for a purpose, but that's explained up ahead. Do not discount anyone who comes into your life.

The only way to interpret any vision or dream is to allow the Holy Spirit to do it for you. In Genesis and Daniel, God gave the dreams to the leaders and no one in the land could interpret them except those God chose to impart His wisdom on to give the meaning of the dreams.

In John 3:27, it says, "A person cannot receive one thing unless it is given to him from Heaven." There is no other way. No man or pastor, apostle or prophet can interpret a dream unless the meaning comes from the Holy Spirit Himself.

There are some visions and dreams that are literal so it is important to have one-on-one alone time with the Lord so He can reveal these things to you. Don't rush it, take your time, sometimes it may take days, weeks or even months for the Lord to reveal the interpretation. We must be willing to wait on Him. There have been visions where He has said if I did not warn them, this literally would happen to them.

Warnings to others can come in different ways. There is the literal way of telling them, but some people won't accept and receive you telling them something bad is going to happen to them. That is not for you to worry about, though. If the Holy Spirit guides you to tell them, then tell them. Sometimes, we are to warn them and leave the rest up to God. It's not our responsibility to ensure they receive it, that's His job. We are to be obedient.

The other way to warn them is the strongest way. It is intercessory prayer by getting on your hands and knees, and standing in the gap for this person. Ask

Jesus, the Holy Spirit, and the Father for this person to receive what you are going to say and or praying that the bad thing you are seeing will be rerouted, stopped and the enemies plan be cancelled.

Paul says in Thessalonians, we are to intercede for others against whatever is coming against them, and whatever the enemy has planned for them to be harmed. We are to pray fervently and ask God to not allow this to happen. There is nothing more wonderful than to pray and war for someone and see them protected, and they do not even know it.

There have been people who have given a prophetic word about an event happening. When it doesn't happen, people think it means they were wrong. No, it means they prayed right. Moses prostrated Himself for the Israelites so God would not destroy them. Moses interceded for God's people.

Many tragic events were altered and stopped from happening because someone was called to war in prayer for that tragedy not to happen.

I wonder how many people have prayed for you without you knowing it and you have been able to dodge disaster because of their prayer.

Sin is missing the mark; intercessory prayer is hitting the target head on with a bullseye every time. As you pray, ask the Holy Spirit to increase and your flesh to decrease. Seek Him in everything you do, and you will not miss the target!

On one of my many Father-daughter dates with God, Jesus, and His Holy Spirit spoke to my spirit, "My daughter, do you know why it is so important My people obey Me?"

I said, "Because You're Almighty God."

He said, "My daughter, it's not because I need people to obey Me, it's much greater than that. I need people to obey because if they don't, many peoples' lives are at risk. The ones who hear Me and don't obey, stand in the way of many miracles and blessings including their own. If I tell you to go tell a woman standing in line at the mall I love her, or the money is coming, or the answer is YES, or she has a purpose, I will give it to you in front of her to let her know it is Me talking. If you didn't go up to her when I tell you to, she could go home and end her life. All it would have taken was someone to say a few select words I would give that would have saved her and saved many others attached to her destiny. You see, My daughter, it is a chain reaction. When I ask something of you, big or small, it all leads to many people being saved and being set free. Therefore, it is so important My people learn and obey My voice."

I was filled with so much emotion, as He reminded me of the previous assignments, He's given me, where I felt uncomfortable doing what He asked, but I just knew in my spirit they were important messages. He never let me go too long with my questions being unanswered.

I realized He was showing me I was done with the smaller tasks, and I was ready for the bigger ones. From that day on, His assignments became more frequent, and more boldness was required of me. He often reminded me, "My grace is sufficient for you for My power is made perfect in weakness" (2 Corinthians 12:9 ESV). I kept replaying the night He told me why it is so important every time He asked me to do something, even if I was fearful, to push through it and I did it.

I spoke, I went and delivered messages, I was able to tell people what they were praying for in their alone time, I was able to see their heart-felt prayers, and know what they needed. I could see what was oppressing them. I could see their dreams. He gave me specific details no one could have known or guessed.

Though the thoughts going through my head said, "This is crazy, how did I know that," He confirmed I was in the right place at the right time, and I was giving the exact message from Him they needed. Their response was usually tears, falling to their knees praising Jesus, and hugging me. The main question was, "How do you know that?" I always answered their questions by giving all the glory to God, Jesus, and the Holy Spirit. These encounters would end many times with me praying with them. His Holy Spirit would speak more through me during the prayers.

I want to be clear. God is the creator of all things. Satan cannot create. He takes what God made perfect and beautiful and he perverts and twists it. We give way too much credit to the enemy for visions, dreams, wisdom, and knowledge. Anyone who is in the occult has allowed the enemy to pervert the gifts they received from God. The enemy cannot create these gifts.

For example, no one could interpret the nightmares and dreams of Pharaoh and King Nebuchadnezzar, except the ones God chose to tell the meaning. God sent the dreams, not the enemy. Satan is called the deceiver for a reason. He can't create, has no authority, and must get permission from God as he did with Job and even Judas. We give way too much credit to the enemy. In Jude1:10 "But those people blaspheme all that they do not understand,.." Very many people come against God's power and His ways because they do not understand it. His word is clear, His ways are not ours. People have put God in a box when He is the infinite transcendent Almighty God that can do the impossible. He is the creator the devil is the imitator.

None of what God was doing through me would have been possible if I had not spent alone time with Him to learn His voice and been patient and grow in our relationship. I sought Him out for everything I needed, even in the small things. I am one vessel among many.

As exciting as it is when He starts giving us increased wisdom and knowledge, we must remain humble and remember this is not for us, this is all for Him and

His glory. It is Him working through us. If we think any of this is our doing, our pride can block the gifts and being able to hear Him clearly. I have seen this happen before.

Ask Yourself...

> *Can He trust me?*
> *Can He trust I will remain humble?*
> *Can He trust I will not steal His glory?*

I still had to fight pride in other situations, but when it came to Him using my vessel, I was humbled more every time I was sent by the Lord to help these people. There are many people who work for the enemy, whether they know it or not, they are sent to harm. In God's Word in 1 John, it says to test the spirit in everything.

Do not allow just anyone to prophesy over your life. The enemy does not know all like the Holy Spirit does. When the Holy Spirit would send me to give messages, I did not ask them any questions. I did not even ask them for their names usually, until I was done giving them the message and had finished praying. God would reveal their name to me at times. Sometimes, I would hear it at the end of our encounter. I did not ask for anything in return nor did I go up to everyone, only the ones He told me to approach. He taught me to move with intention.

I was also used as the confirmer. There were many times someone in their past had told them something similar, they saw it, read it, dreamt it, or heard from a family member, or church pastor or was given to them in the word of God when they were reading the Bible. They would tell me it was a thought that kept occupying their mind. God would use me to confirm what people were questioning and or seeking Him in. Many were at a crossroads in their life and were waiting to hear from Him.

Will everyone's walk be like mine? Of course not.

Will your assignments be the same as mine? No.

Will He ask you to do things out of your comfort zone? Absolutely.

Will He use you in ways you could never imagine? Yes.

Will He ask you to do things that go against the grain and will cause others to call you crazy, mock you, and persecute you? Yes.

However, what is so great about being persecuted is when you live your life for Jesus Christ and allow the Holy Spirit to lead the way, He shows you things that will blow your mind and you no longer care what the world says. All you want to do is go deeper in Him and go where He will take you. It literally and truly is out of this world and worth anything people can throw at you. Jesus said that they will hate us, but to never forget they hated Him first. It's an honor to be persecuted and mocked for Jesus Christ sake.

Ask Yourself...

Can you think back to a time where you felt a nudge to help someone or call someone to check on them?

What did you do?

How about a time where you heard a whisper, don't go out tonight, or don't go to that place, stay home?

What did you do?

That was the Holy Spirit. Reading this book is a divine appointment. I know the Holy Spirit has talked with you already whether you knew it or not. This book is His voice through me, telling you He wants to take you deeper and bring you freedom in Jesus Christ. It's your appointed time!

Continue to invite Him into your space and your life.

During what I call my second level assignment season, He sent me on back-to-back assignments, and

I often had assignments every day, sometimes multiple times a day, and, at times, across the nation.

I was serving at my church, and His request for me was to join the prayer team and serve. He instructed me not to hold back, take extra shifts, stay longer, and pray for as many people as I could.

"I will send the rights ones to you," He told me.

I served my heart out, and after many months of nonstop serving for my church, He transitioned me and had me learn what a church without walls meant. He said me and others like me were the church. It was not about walls or a building. Many people won't ever step into church, but we were to be the church for many of His people.

I was still carrying anger and struggling with stubbornness, but that did not stop Him from using me. I want to keep pointing out my brokenness along the way, and the layers and time it took to reach my full walk-in freedom in Jesus. However, the more I sought and the more I knocked, the more He kept giving me.

One vision I love recalling is when He told me to stop and pull my car over to watch what He was going to reveal to me. That was when I saw the army of God in Heaven. All His people were dressed in different colored armor. In this vision, I saw each set of colors, and when they were all together in Heaven, they looked like the rainbow. I was flooded with revelation of knowing what each color represented. For example, the prophets wore royal blue and gold. The apostles were in bright red and gold, and the preachers were all in sparkling silver. I saw the warriors at the gates of Hell, and they were in solid gold. I saw the Evangelists in bright yellow and silver and the teachers were in orange and gold. I saw the healers and mercy carriers in green and purple. I saw much more, but I can't put words into what He showed me. I was able to pinpoint what each person was by what color they wore. When I would see someone, the Holy Spirit would lift the veil and I would see these people with their colored armor on. I would be stunned at first but became accustomed to seeing it. Even if the person was not a follower; I saw who they would become if they were following Jesus. I would be flooded with seeing their purpose, and what they would do if they walked in alignment with God.

I could be on the phone with someone, and immediately a vision would come to me, and I was able to see who I was talking to, what anointing they carried and what gifts God bestowed upon them. I could see their struggle and their past just by hearing their voice. It was unreal. It was God and His Holy Spirit. He never gave me insight for me, He gave it to bring redemption to His people and to prove God was always with them. He saw it all and He wanted them.

Each one of God's people is anointed. However, not everyone is anointed with the same anointing or gifts from the Holy Spirit. One mistake I have seen others make is to compare their anointing, gifts and calling to mine or anyone else's. Don't feel your anointing, gifts or calling are less or better. In Ephesians 4:16, Paul wrote, "He makes the whole body fit together perfectly. As each part does its own special work, it helps the other parts grow, so that the whole body is healthy and growing and full of love." You're anointing, the gifts and calling He gives you are tailored for you, but they fit perfectly with mine and all others who are a part of the Body of Christ so we can serve effectively in the Kingdom of God. We must remember these anointings, gifts and callings are for His glory and His glory alone. They are used so we can be servants to our fellow brothers and sisters in Christ. We are to use them with honor and reverence. We are to use them to build His Kingdom. They are not for us to boast about.

If you could see the most common pattern in my walk, it was my alone time with His Holy Spirit. My alone time was crucial to my walk and my relationship with Him.

Your alone time with Him will be what determines how deep He can and will take you.

Ask Yourself...

> *With everything I am carrying, wouldn't it be nice, to let Him carry it for me?*

_____

Would it help to know I don't have to do this life alone?

_____

Do I now realize I was never created to live this life alone?

_____

If God is showing me a dream or a vision over and over, what is He trying to tell me? Write down any scriptures that come to mind after asking this question.

_____

What is the best way for me to warn someone of a vision nor dream God has given me about them?

_____

Why it is so important God's people read His word and learn to obey His voice?

_____

Remember, pray, and ask God to reveal His purpose for every dream or vision He gives you before you talk to anyone else about it. If you still feel you don't know ask Him to give you scriptures that pertain to what He is trying to reveal to you. Don't rush ahead of Him.

"Fight your battles through prayer;
And win your battles through faith."

– Luffina Lourdura[6]

―――――――――――――――
[6] Goodreads.com

Chapter 6

Spiritual Warfare

When it comes to spiritual warfare, this is a topic I could spend a whole book on. However, I am going to stick to what is most important to ensure you stay ready and protected on our daily walk against spiritual warfare.

First, we have to get used to it. Spiritual warfare will come at us our entire lives. The enemy hates what God loves. He wants to pervert it and destroy it. He comes to kill, steal, and destroy, but Jesus came to give life and give it abundantly. The enemy wants to steal what Jesus has given us and destroy our life so it will lead to a path of death.

Once we accept the fact we are God's chosen ones, His beloved children and warfare comes, we will be able to withstand the enemy attacks. The best way to come against the enemy is by God's Word. God's Word is life. It says in Hebrews 4:12, His Word is alive and active, and it is sharper than any double-edged sword. It can pierce through soul and spirit, and cut through bone and marrow. We must be equipped with it, and we must use it.

Every morning, I strongly encourage you to put on the spiritual armor Paul speaks about in Ephesians 6:10-18. When we do not put on the spiritual armor, it is the same as a soldier walking out on the battlefield with no weapons and no gear. I have gone days in the past where I missed a day putting my armor on and I saw a clear distinction versus when I would put the armor of God on.

In the Word it says our weapons are not carnal, they are mighty in God for pulling down strongholds. Strongholds are mindsets. When we are going to be fighting spiritual warfare, we cannot use flesh weapons. Many people are trying to control situations, or fight them in the flesh only to see them backfire.

We are not fighting the flesh.

God's Word is alive and holds power. When we speak it to the enemy, it demolishes the attacks.

Stop right now, pray out loud, and put on your armor.

Father, please forgive me of every sin, unknown and known. I place the helmet of salvation over my head to protect my mind from the enemy and that I would hear your Holy Spirit above all voices. I place the breast plate of righteousness over my heart, to guard my heart and I ask You to help me walk in righteousness. My feet are shod with the preparation of peace, and I will speak the gospel wherever I go. I am at peace no matter what storm arises against me. I carry the sword of the spirit in my right-hand speaking "It is written." I carry the shield of faith in my left hand to quench the fiery darts of the enemy and I bind up all attacks coming against me, my family, and my destiny. Lastly, I place the belt of truth around my waist. Jesus you are the way the truth and the life. Amen.

The Weapon of Prayer

Before any prayer, you must repent of all known and all unknown sins. If you want your prayer to be effective, you must believe what you are praying for, and you must have a sincere heart.

One of the things that makes prayer extremely powerful is using the Word of God in your prayers. God loves it when you give Him back His Word. Example: If God has made you a promise but it seems you are far from it, or there seems to be many things trying to stop you, you can recite these verses. Isaiah 55:11 says, "Lord God, Your Word never returns to You void," and in 2 Corinthians 1:20 it says, "For all the promises of God find their yes in Him." You can give His Word back to Him and let Him know you believe in Him for what He is doing.

In God's Word it says, we have been given authority through Jesus Christ. Anything we ask in His name, our Father will give it to us (see John 14:13-17).

The Holy Spirit lifts the veil for the benefit of His children. When we start to ask God for His will over our life, when we fall to our knees and say, "I give up my choices, I want what You want for me. I want Your will for my life. My life is not my own. I am not here to do my will but yours Lord." We have hit a maturity in the spirit that allows us to not fear what is next.

Turn Around Time

I was called back to Utah, the place where I made the most selfish decision of my life. It was what led to this storm in the first place. It was also where the guy I left my ex-husband for lived. When I would go visit him, I would feel depressed and sad. I did not like being there. Our Father intended for me to go back to face what I had done and to close that chapter in my life for good. I did not want to admit to myself what that meant, but I knew it had to be done, no matter what or who I lost.

I got to Utah on August 1 and heard Him say, "Meet Me in the mountains." I went up and hiked, and before I knew it was getting dark. I started to head back down, and came to a turn. I didn't ask Him which way, I just let my feet go to the left and thought this would get me back to my car. An hour later, I was still walking back and realized I went the wrong way. Two hours later in the dark, I made it down. However, I was on the other side of the mountain, and I had to call an Uber to come and get me.

After I returned home, I asked our Father, "What happened?"

He said, "My daughter, you didn't ask Me, nor did you pay attention. This season I am going to need you to pay attention to what I am going to be showing you."

That night I had a dream. I got lost and had to spend the night in the wilderness by myself. I was alone and scared. I woke up worried, and then I heard, "Good morning, My daughter, today is going to be a great day. Get dressed and meet me on Provo mountain."

I looked up the mountain He wanted me to go to and I headed out. I got there and it said it was a two-mile hike up and a two-mile hike down. It was around 9 a.m. I thought, no big deal, I will be back after lunch.

At the end of the hike, there was a beautiful waterfall. I stood under it a minute and heard His Spirit say to me, "Take the other way down." There were only two ways down, the way I came up or going to my right, which looked like it was going to lead me back to my car.

As I began to head down the way He instructed me to go, I realized I was going to have to climb straight down on sharp rocks. As I was climbing down, it felt like there was no end to them. I paused and heard, "Keep going." I kept going and two hours later, I was still going. I stopped. I was thankful I had my headphones playing praise music to keep me at peace. I made it to the end of the rocks, only to see a stream of water with broken down trees all over it. There was no other way to get around it. I would have to crawl through the branches and broken trees. The water was ice cold. I had on sandals, hiking pants, and a tank top. I was cold and very tired. I started to break down and cry.

I heard His voice, "My daughter, you're almost there."

I held on to that. After another few hours, though, I was exhausted and wanted to quit.

I hear again, "You're almost there."

With tears streaming down my face, I yelled out, "You keep saying that!"

I was cold and just wanted to be back home. Regretting coming this way and questioning if I heard Him right. I sat down to rest, and I heard Him say, "My daughter, pay attention."

I looked around me, and I saw orange peels and empty water bottles. Immediately, I had newfound energy. I saw someone else had done this hike, so that meant I could, too. I kept going. What was supposed to be an easy hike turned into an eleven-hour trek. I only had a few oranges and a couple water bottles. I didn't eat before I left because I thought I would be back by lunch and would eat then.

I kept going and I finally was able to reach the bottom. I was so happy. Then, a sudden realization I was in the middle of nowhere. It was getting late and my dream from the night before came crashing back to me.

I fell to my knees and begged Him, "Dad please, please, don't leave me out here all alone, with no protection."

After a few minutes of complete silence from Him, He said, "What did I tell you, pay attention."

I took my headphones out and started to look and listen. I heard women laughing. I started to run quickly to where I heard the voices coming from. I reached the area where I heard the women laughing and it was the start of the hike. I was blown away. I stood there in complete shock, falling to me knees laughing and crying.

I heard His Spirit speak to me, "My daughter, that hike was a representation of your life without Me. You took the hard way, but I was still able to get you back to where you started to give you a second chance to do it all over again."

I went home that night in complete wonder.

The next day, I was awakened with, "Good morning, My daughter, today is going to be an easier day. Meet Me at your favorite lake."

My favorite lake was Silver Lake, up near Brighton Ski resort in Utah. It had a board walk, and it was a nice lake to take a stroll around. I started to walk and allowed the breeze to hit my face.

I heard His Holy Spirit say, "My daughter, do you see how smooth this walk is"?

I said, "Yes, Dad, I do."

He said to me, "This is how the rest of your life will be with Me leading you. You won't have to worry about anything. Lean on me and I will guide you in the paths of righteousness. Your worst days are behind you."

He was right, of course. However, that didn't mean in the flesh the days up head looked easier. What He meant was no matter what, I had Him. He was going to help me though every situation. My perception wouldn't see them as the worse days, I would see them as an opportunity to learn and become stronger in Him.

There were many more tests up ahead, but each one was going to lead to one less bondage I had to carry.

Understanding the Armor of God

Read Ephesians 6:11-13.

List each part of the armor.
Then explain how you are to use it.

Sample Prayers

Use these prayers to get you started using scripture-filled prayers during your spiritual warfare.

> *Father, please forgive me for all my sins and all my unknown sins. Father, in Your Word it says we are to enter Your courts with thanksgiving and praise. I thank You, Father for all the many blessings You have given me. I know Your ways are not my ways and Your thoughts are not my thoughts. Help me to posture my heart in ways that are pleasing to You. Father, You bring the rod to the wicked, but You love a humble heart. My heart, soul and lips will forever bless you.*

> *Father, God, may Your Holy Spirit increase in me as my flesh decreases. I know no weapon formed against me will prosper, and every tongue that rises up against me will be refuted. I know the weapons of warfare are not of the flesh, but have divine power to destroy strongholds. I take every thought captive and bring it under obedience to You.*

I know Father, You have plans to prosper me and give me hope for my future. I know You anoint my head with oil and You are leading beside still waters. You are my shepherd, and I shall not want for anything.

I know Father if I abide in You and You abide in me, I know anything I ask for You will give me. Help to replace the desires of my heart with the desires You have for me, I know You formed me in my mother's womb, and You have numbered all of my days. I ask and receive Your grace and peace over my life.

I know in John it says no one receives even one thing unless it comes from heaven, I know everything I have is from You and I am grateful for all that You do. As I continue to abide under the shadow of Your wings, You will guard me and protect me and charge Your angels to watch over me.

Father, in Your Word it says we can come boldly to Your throne, and with You nothing is impossible and whatever we bind or loose in heaven, it is bound and loosed on earth. By the blood of the Lamb,

I bind up any demonic attack or spirits coming against me, my family, or my destiny. I loosen all the blessings You have ordained over my life, and I speak life into every dead thing in my life that needs to be resurrected. Resurrection power lives within me.

Father, I trust You and I am to be still and know that You are God, I know You will fight all my battles for me, for the battle belongs to the You. Father, when my enemies come against me, I will pray for them, forgive them, and ask You to bless them. Father, I know You tell me not to try to pay back an enemy, that vengeance belongs to You.

Father, I declare and decree that the enemy has lost all legal rights to my life and to my destiny. I speak life over me and over everything that concerns me. Thank You, even though I do not understand everything, I will lean not on my own understanding but in all my ways I will acknowledge You. I know You are the lamp unto my feet. I will not dwell on the former things because I know You are doing a new thing in my life and in and through me. I seek to have more wisdom to bring you glory.

Thank You, Lord, for I know I can do all things through Christ who strengthens me. I declare and decree victory over me and my life. I love You, Abba, Father, my life is not for me, it is for You, Your Holy Spirit, and Your Son Jesus Christ. I loosen the fruits of the Spirit over me. Help me to continue to walk in love and be this world's salt and light and the hands and feet of Jesus Christ, in Jesus mighty name, Amen.

Another way to use the written Word is to take a verse like Psalm 91 for example: "Those who live under the shelter of the most high will find rest in the shadow of the Almighty."

You can then take it and personalize it: "I, Natasha, who lives under the shelter of the most high, will find rest in the shadow of the Almighty.

Another example is from Galatians 6:9, "I, Natasha will not grow weary in doing good for in due season I will reap a harvest if I do not give up." I, Natasha can do all things through Christ who strengthens me."

"Behold, to obey is better than sacrifice…"

(1 Samuel 15:22 ESV)

Chapter 7

Choosing Obedience

Obedience is a daily choice to humble yourself, surrender all, and allow Him to lead you even if it's the way no one else is going.

It's giving Him our full yes and not taking it back even when it gets uncomfortable or hard. As Kingdom kids, we must be willing to fight the voices of the world and of the enemy. We must be willing to choose Him and His way every time. Obedience leads to freedom, even though it can cause us to go against the grain, and to stand up when everyone says to sit down.

I wake up every day with my mind made up that no matter what He asks of me, even if I am scared, don't agree with it, fear it will lead to a loss in my life, or feel it's going to cause people to mock me, I still will do it. It is a discipline that takes time to develop.

There were many days I didn't feel like it, but the feelings did not trump the discipline and the fear of letting my Father down. I loved hearing, "Well done, I am proud of you." I did not want to disobey because I loved Him so much and I loved how He loved me.

I have read and believe obedience is greater than sacrifice. I want to add I truly believe we must be willing to sacrifice our wants and our flesh to have a postured heart to be willing to walk out a life in obedience.

Obedience is a commitment. We have to be willing to trust when He asks us to do something. When He asked me to do some things, I was afraid, filled with doubt, and had so many "what ifs" like, what if they laugh at me or call me crazy. My desire to please the Lord and help people overpowered any fear of rejection or persecution.

Many people quote the verse, He will give you the desires of your heart from Psalm 37:4. We live in a fallen world, where feelings and emotions deceive you. Where magazines, books, and social media tell us what we should want. What I have come to find out in my walk is we must read the entire verse and "delight ourselves in the Lord," meaning we align ourselves with the Word of God and with His will in our life. Our desires start to be traded in for His desires for us. He is our creator, therefore, He knows exactly what we need and what will allow us to fulfill our purpose and live out a life that is fulfilling in Christ.

What does that look like for you?
Are there things you can recall you know
He asked you to do and you didn't out of
fear or doubt it was Him saying it?

God will never ask you to do something that does not align with His Word. Always test the spirit and seek the word and Him in everything you do. If it is condemning or bringing you anxiety, you may not be hearing Him right, get alone with the Father every day. He brings peace when He calls us to do something for His glory even if it is uncomfortable.

Many people ask me, "What about my family and my responsibilities?"

I tell them, in order to love your family, and to properly steward your responsibilities, you need to have God in the center of all of it. His Holy Spirit is the one who will guide you in all things.

Spending time with God:

- ➢ Wake up early to ensure you get alone time with Him.
- ➢ Turn off the TV, computer, or phone to read the Word or praise and worship Him.
- ➢ Talk and pray in the car, on the way to work or home.
- ➢ Throughout the day, make Him your number one priority in every decision.

➤ Before you do anything, ask Him, "Is this what You want for me, Father?".

➤ Be willing to wait on Him and obey what He tells you even if the answer is not what you want to hear.

As I continued to put this discipline to work, I was able to ask Him for answers to questions and be ready for whatever the answer. Sometimes I would hear, "No, not good idea." Being me, I would ask why. Sometimes He would give me an answer, and other times, He would tell me I didn't need to concern myself with the why, just trust Him. When His Holy Spirit would give me a reason, it was usually a "wow" moment. Other times I would hear, "They don't have good intentions, or I am protecting you from something." I was quickened in my spirit and would obey. I have become stronger in not needing to know why anymore. I trust everything He has done for me, why should I doubt Him now?

As we start to make Him the center of every decision, it then allows us to know more and see more. He will help us stay out of trouble. Whereas in the past, I would walk into a trap, situation or a relationship that would take a long time to recover from. He truly helps us stay on a path of righteousness.

When I was told to go to the back of the line, or when He told me to speak to the woman in the courthouse, those were examples of how important obedience is.

Obedience is greater than just us. We truly step into serving our brothers and sisters when we walk in complete obedience to Him.

Delivery

When we start to hear the Holy Spirit, the enemy can come quickly and try to pervert it. I have made this mistake and gotten prideful thinking because I hear God and He tells me something about someone and how they were wrong, it's my place to jump ahead of Him and tell them what the Father is telling me.

There will be more times than not what we are hearing is for us to pray for or to be aware of, and not to be repeated until an appointed time. There are also times, where He does want us to deliver a message. However, if we are still walking with some pride, we may deliver it in the wrong way. All that does is push people away and no one is going to want to hear what the Lord has to say through us. No one person is greater than the other. There may be some people who have a calling requiring more responsibility, but they are not better. We are to continue to remember, we need to walk in humility and the fruits of the Holy Spirit.

When we deliver messages from the Almighty God, even if it is a warning, we need to do it with gentleness. We need to have compassion and walk in His love.

Remember, in Matthew 12:36 it says we must account for every idle word we will ever speak. Make sure what we are speaking is spoken to bring harmony, redemption and love, not, "I am better than you." Every word we speak is also a seed planted that will one day be harvested. No matter what, we will reap everything we sow; good or bad.

As followers of Christ, we know the truth. The truth is the truth no matter who it offends, and we must stand boldly for the truth. However, everyone comes from different walks in life, and someone could come to Christ if we would take the time to listen to them instead of shutting them down. We have to remove the thought they don't have anything to say because they are wrong or don't believe the way we do.

We have to ask the Holy Spirit to remove our pride, or we will push more people away from the Kingdom then bring them in. These are people God chose us to usher into His Kingdom.

We are to love as Jesus did, we are to speak the truth but with humility not haughtiness. Father God was quick to tell me when I was in the wrong, however, He did it with authoritative love.

One day, I got into an argument with someone, and when I got in my car and said, "Dad, can You believe that person, wow, they were so wrong."

With all His love and truth, He said, "Well, My daughter, actually you both were wrong, but you know better, they don't. You need to turn around and go back and apologize."

He didn't want me to think I was right when I wasn't, and He didn't want to leave that person with the thought, "This is how God's people act." So, He made me turn around and go back, He guided my thoughts on what to say, and when I was done apologizing, this person let me say what I was trying to say in the first place. This time it was done and spoken in love and to my surprise it was received and led to their salvation.

**We are representations of the Holy Kingdom.
Our actions must mimic the way Jesus acted.**

God wants every part of us. We were made from Him. He took the time to create each of us and our personalities. He knew how we would receive information and how we would act and respond to certain situations. He knows what we need. He is not afraid to let us know when we are in the wrong. He is always seeking us and chasing after us.

One memory, I want to bring you that makes me laugh, but really showed me how much God was not going to give up on me.

Back when my journey of walking a life Christ crucified started, I got a filing from the courts, and it came back with a result I did not want to see. I was angry, I had been hearing, "You will claim victory in My name."

However, all I saw were failures. I had not yet learned I was walking in victory already and His timing was different than the time we expect. I got so upset.

On my way to my car I heard, "My daughter, let's talk through this, nothing is what it seems."

I screamed, "NO, I don't want to talk!"

I got in my car and turned up the radio loud enough to drown out any thoughts and drove very fast down highway 45 in Houston.

Suddenly, I heard a voice so loud I almost swerved my car saying, "You really think I cannot speak to you over this radio? Turn it down NOW and listen to Me."

I was trembling in anger, but mostly fear. I could feel Him and how He was not going to let me act this way.

I turned down the radio, and His voice softened, "My daughter, nothing is what it seems, this will turn around, just watch. Stop focusing on what you see in the flesh, what is unseen is what is eternal, and you have no idea what I have planned for you. Place the weight on Me. I await the day when you find out what all this is for and how many people I will use you to help. Your pain has a true purpose. It's developing great strength and faith. Many people who are attached to you are being set free and I am redeeming time. I am making beauty for ashes. Now, slow down and go back home."

God loves us so much; He will chase us down even on a highway. He will find us where we are and will help us clear away fear and reveal the truth. He gives peace that surpasses all understanding.

Pause and Reflect…

> *Have you wondered how you can know it is God and not just what you want to hear?*_____

My answer is He has spoken things I refused to admit about myself. No one else could have made me stop, no one else would have stayed with me through it. I didn't like myself, so how could I have come up with such love and discipline. I couldn't. I never wanted to admit I was wrong in the past. He would be the one to correct me and teach me. He would speak something specific, and randomly, I would meet someone, and they would say, "God wants me to tell you, "and it would be exactly what He told me in private. God sent me messengers and confirmations through people just as He used me to do.

In His Word it says He will send two or more to confirm His word and He did **every** time. I have seen what He shows me and tells me to tell others come to pass. The details may not look the way we want or be in the timeframe we expect, but the result came back to match what He would say or show me.

Have you done something out of hurt?

Were you emotional or angry?

How could it have helped if our Father helped you see what was really going on?

What I want to point out, if I acted like that with others, they would leave me, and get angry with me. It would cause so much turmoil between us. But with the Father, Jesus Christ, and His Holy Spirit guiding, He walked me through each situation no matter how I was acting, He has never left or forsaken me. He has never made me feel I was less, He waited, He was so patient with me. Yes, He got on me, but I needed His tough love. There was no way I would ever admit the things He showed me about me. I was so ashamed. He sat with me, wiped my tears away, and held my hand all the way through. He chastised me but not one time did He make me feel condemned. He convicted me to want to change.

Brothers and sisters, our Father wants you even when you are broken with your sins, your hidden life, your hurt, and your anger. He wants it, so He can uproot it and replace it. He loves you so much. I know in this moment; you can even feel your body tingling and your heart softening because you feel His encompassing love surround you.

You know you don't deserve it, but none of us do. I didn't. That's what makes His love so real. He gives it anyway. He wants you to draw closer to Him.

Parents, what do we do for our children? We want to protect them, we want to love them, and keep them safe. We want to let them know we are there for them no matter what. We would give our very breath for them. Our Heavenly Father gave us children to show us His love for us. He gave us marriage to show Jesus' love for His church; that's us brothers and sisters. We are His church. We are the Father's children.

Getting more excited, to get to know our Father with a deeper intimacy?

Do you catch yourself asking "Dad, can you hear me? Can we really talk like this? Even after all I have done, you still want a relationship with me?"

The answer is "Yes!" He is excited to speak with you, He is waiting with open arms, run to Him.

"Self-worth is so important to your happiness, if you don't feelgood about yourself, it's hard to feel good about anything else."

– Sandy Hale

Chapter 8

Self-Worth

Delayed Obedience Is Disobedience

There were many times I felt alone on this journey and to the human eye, I was. I knew I had my Dad with me, but as far as people, He didn't let too many stay in my life. I would get temporary seasons where I was able to serve in a church, help others, but I always found myself having to move on without them. Looking back, I now see why. Someone who worked for me gave me the name of a person she said reminded her of me. His name was Terry Looper.

Through my journey, the Holy Spirit was my teacher. He did not let me read other books; He wanted me to focus on the Bible. He wanted most of what I learned to be authentic and from Him. I decided after much prayer to later order Terry Looper's book. When I started to read it, I could feel an instant connection to some of his experiences and how he loved the Lord and how His Holy Spirit led him in everything He did.

As I was seeking some answers to a business idea and how I should go about it, I asked the Lord for some guidance. His Spirit spoke, "Reach out to Terry Looper." I was afraid it was in my flesh, so I went on my way.

During a church service I attended with a friend, the pastor spoke and immediately the Lord spoke to me, "You are blocking your blessing by not listening to Me, delayed obedience is still disobedience."

I want to keep pointing out, I was always questioning if it was my flesh or Him, and He would come in and confirm it was Him. We can't stop our blessings, but we can block them and delay them.

I prayed, stepped out in faith, and wrote Mr. Looper my testimony up to that moment. Exactly twelve hours later, he wrote me back saying he would like to meet with me. As I was preparing for the meeting through prayer, I knew I had three months before we met. I used each day to pray for the meeting, that it would be prosperous, Mr. Looper would receive me, and I would receive him.

As the day approached, His Holy Spirit told me, "My daughter, Mr. Looper is going to have a message for you from Me that will forever change the trajectory of your life, how you will run future businesses, and will change who you are."

I thought, "Wow, I wonder what that means."

I got to my meeting with Mr. Looper, and immediately we both recognized we walked with the Lord guiding our steps. He knew in his spirit I was there because I was walking in obedience.

After talking about what brought us to that moment in life, I told him one of my struggles about promoting the nonprofit I was led to open.

His response to me was, "It is not a money issue. It is a self-worth issue and problem."

God knew I would not have been able to accept that from anyone else. In that moment of complete truth and clarity, His Spirit told me I was operating on temporary confidence, but had zero self-worth. I still didn't know who I was in Christ. Even though I was helping many and seeing what God was doing, I didn't have my worth anchored in Him.

I knew what He told me I was anointed with, and I knew the many gifts He had given me. I knew parts of the calling on my life, but none of those were my identity. I was about to step into finding out my worth was in Him.

Even when we think we are doing good, He will keep surprising us and revealing hidden areas we need to deal with. The next months ahead were brutal. I thought I had already gone through the emotional arena when I finally got rid of anger and stubbornness; two of my biggest areas of bondage. I was able to keep my emotions under His control and I was walking in the fruits of the Spirit and focusing on a consistent walk with kindness. I wanted to help and love His people.

This however, was an indicator that I was ready to tackle this final hidden area all the other spirits could attach themselves to; thus shutting down their ability to spread to other areas of my life.

Again, I was called back to our sacred space behind the cross. He told me to buy a brand-new journal, meet Him, and be ready. "I am going to take you all the way back to the beginning," He said.

Through the next months, He took me back to the main events in my life, starting from when I was two. Even though I had suppressed many painful memories, He walked with me back into each memory. I was able to see Him holding my little hand. He showed me what was done or said that chipped away at my identity and worth. He never left me. He allowed me to see and hear some painful things all the way to that point in my journey. Sometimes, He spent days with me on one memory. There were times I didn't want to go back. I didn't want to face what I had buried so deep. The pain was too much for me at times. He would keep reminding me of the years I had already conquered with Him. I couldn't quit. I had to finish.

Through each moment He took me back to, He walked me though what was really happening. People say there are two sides to every story, but each person recalls an event by their own perception. I believe there are three sides to every story, each of our sides and the truth. Jesus showed me the truth. He showed me and allowed me to feel and have the wisdom to see what the others involved were feeling. What amazed me about each event was not one had to do with me. When I was three, the adults' feelings were not my fault. When I was eight, their pain had gone much further back than my eight-year-old self. When I was three, four, and nine, I was an innocent child. Each person I gave a piece of me had everything to do with what they were battling, facing, and the heavy burdens they were carrying.

After months of those severe sessions and encounters of my purifying process with His Holy Spirit and my Dad, I found my self-worth in Him.

He then began to take me back to events in my life where I misunderstood situations. He showed me my mom's heart and her struggles. The truth He revealed was all the sacrifices my mom made for me and my brothers and how she went without to ensure we had what we needed. What she was doing, although hidden and misunderstood by me, was what kept me alive. He showed me how she gave her best with what she had and tried to have my best interest. Because I was already struggling with wounds (from when I was younger that had nothing to do with her), I projected my pain onto her. This caused me to blame her and become angry with her, even comparing her to other moms on TV. While my behavior was not justified, I felt very misunderstood by her.

I set her up to fail in my eyes because I didn't know how to be set free from all my pain and the internal battle I was facing every day. I didn't know how to express what I was struggling with except through resentment and mean words. I blamed her for my pain. My pain turned into rebellion and disrespect. She would stand up to me as she dealt with her own battles. We went in a vicious cycle of me feeling justified in my behavior of treating her disrespectfully. I blamed her for everything. Both of us were operating in the flesh and not knowing what was happening in the spirit realm, made for a chaotic upbringing.

I used to wonder how my mom knew things, such as when I was hanging around someone who might hurt or harm me. As children, we want to be right, and we want to say our parents don't understand us, forgetting they used to be us.

What God revealed to me was He gave us our parents. They are gifts, just as children are gifts to their parents. He chose our parents especially for us. Even if we are adopted, God chose each parent for their child. He gave them the ability to guide them. Whether the child chooses to receive the guiding is up to them which is just like our relationship with our Father in Heaven.

He imparts wisdom to parents only available from Him. Whether a parent chooses to listen to

God's wisdom is their choice. My mom listened to His wisdom without even realizing it and she knew exactly when someone was going to be trouble in my life. Me, being stubborn and prideful, mixed with a parent doing things to keep her daughter safe, and the enemy having access to my thoughts due to my pride and hurt, he deceived me and blinded me. By the enemy blinding me, it allowed a much more damaging door to be open, anger and internal rage. When anger came, it brought lack of control, and it spiraled down from there. I had let the enemy deceive me saying my mom was my enemy.

Jesus and the Holy Spirit (bringer of truth) searches everything and even reveals God's secrets (see 1Corinthians 2:10). They took me layer-by-layer and peeled back every lie and revealed the truth of each situation and event. With each revelation, I felt freer, less burdened, and excited to have a fresh new look at my life.

I also wept and prayed for my mom. At this time, she and I weren't talking. We would talk, but then go many months even years without talking.

There were many other events in my life, having nothing to do with my mom, that were painful when the truth was revealed. His Spirit brought comfort and gave me everything I needed to get through this season.

Ask Yourself...

Was there a time when my mom or dad gave me words of wisdom and I didn't listen, then something happened, and they were proven to be right? _____

How did that situation end up? [Typesetter insert 2 lines]

Do I wish I could go back and not get in that relationship or make that decision my parent advised or warned me against?

How many times has my Heavenly Father tried to keep me out of trouble, but I've let the enemy deceive me by telling me my way is better? (Man's wisdom is foolish.)

If you are struggling with forgiving a parent, I ask you to find a place and ask Jesus and the Holy Spirit to meet you there and take you back and reveal the truth to you. Ask Him to help you forgive, and give you eyes to see them the way Jesus does.

Thankfully, two years later my mom came back into my life, and I was able to show her just how much I loved her, and appreciated her for all she did. I showed her just how sorry I was by serving her. The Lord used me to not only have the privilege of baptizing my mom but also, He used me as a vessel to help her grow in His word and in intimacy with Him. My mom was able to learn and experience firsthand, what He had taught me through my walk with Him. I got a second chance to be the daughter she deserved, and together, we got to experience a healthy mother/daughter relationship; which is stronger today than it ever has been. I look at who we have both become in Jesus, and the amount of spiritual growth we have done. I watched Him set her completely free. No one can tell me that God is not alive. He truly restores the years the locust ate up.

My Heavenly Father knew I was going to need to forgive myself and repent for how I treated my mom if I was going to be a good parent where my children would love and respect me.

Looking back at this time in my life, I didn't see my daughters too much. They had moved to another state, and even though I wanted to fight it, the Holy Spirit made it clear I was to let them go for a time. I knew why. These seasons with the Holy Spirit were back-to-back, and although freeing, they were exhausting. Afterwards, all I wanted to do was go home, sleep, and be ready to get up and come back to tackle another lie from the enemy and have Him reveal the truth.

Pause and Reflect

If you are ready to face the past so you can move forward, consider letting the great counselor come in and walk with you and heal you. If you have been to therapy and still feel there is something missing, this will be life changing. Be patient as He reveals the truth to you.

Get a new journal and write down those memories that haunt you, hurt you, and you can't seem to let go.

Write down when you were hurt, when you felt rejected, when you were abandoned, and anything you can remember about these events.

Now, ask the Holy Spirit to reveal areas where you are hurting and may not even know it. Ask Jesus to hold your hand as He reveals truth to you.

Even if you think you have dealt with it, you truly haven't been healed fully unless you have let Him walk with you through it and uproot it. Nothing can compare to what God will do in those moments. This will be life changing.

Sit on the floor or however you sit in surrender to Him. Put your palms up to release to Him your burdens, put on praise and worship music to be ushered into His courts. Have your journal open on the floor and record what He shows you.

A brother in Christ asked me, "What if He doesn't show up?"

I told him, "You must remove the fear and doubt by asking Him to remove any blockage."

God will never disappoint. Seek Him and sit in His presence. You have to be ready. This is not easy. It's painful, and there are some doors you may not even be able to open yet because you may need to gain clarity into other areas of your life and forgive others first before you can see more in depth into another situation.

Pray: *Abba, Father, I want to know You in a more intimate way. I want this relationship to be more. You know I am struggling to see You in this way, so Father help me. Break down what is blocking me, uproot what is stopping me and hurting me. Prune out everything getting in the way of seeing Your love and Your truth. Hold my hand as we go back to the memory You want me to see.*

Be ready! He is going to give you truth and knowledge in so many ways, not just in your mind, but in your heart, mind, soul, and spirit. He is going to show up in so many ways it is going to be overwhelming, and you will be exhausted, but each morning you will wake up freer.

This same brother in Christ, called me later after doing as I suggested and told me Jesus showed up. Since then, I have seen Him freer and more at peace.

As He takes you back, He is going to flood your mind with knowledge and the understanding of what was going on in your situation. He is going to show you every part of the situation. You are going to be flooded with tears, but don't fight them. Let the Holy Spirit clean out what has been holding you back all these years. Run to Him! Your freedom is waiting.

God always answers prayers.
He says Yes, No, or Wait.

When His answer is wait, we often rebel. The waiting period can be a great blessing, though.

Will you take Him up on His offer even
when He says, yes, but wait? ___

If there is something God is making you wait for but has promised you, hold tight and work your wait. This means seek God and ask Him to reveal anything within you that offends Him and needs to be uprooted. There may be things you didn't know were there.

Realize, when God gives us a promise, there is the promise, the preparation, then there is the harvest as the promise comes to pass. If God were to give us all the blessings at one time, and we haven't prepared for it, we could squander it. A blessing at the wrong time could be a curse. The preparation time teaches us how we are going to steward our blessing, how to have gratitude, and allows us to look back and see all God did through us.

Note: The other part of the waiting and preparation part of the process is not just about you, it's the others involved, too. For example, if God tells you He has your kingdom spouse, yet this person is still stuck in their sin, if you two got together out of God's timing, it could end in disaster. You wouldn't know how to appreciate each other or how to discern spiritual warfare, so you'd start to resent each other. It would be over before it ever started.

However, if you wait, prepare, and allow God to refine and teach you, when the appointed hour comes and you join together as one, you are going to both love and appreciate each other with Him as your center. He will help you both steward your responsibilities in the relationship to help it proposer and grow. You two will have the blueprint from what He took you through while you were waiting for the promise to come to pass.

What you do in your single life will carry into your married life. Therefore, it is important to put God in the center of everything you do. It works the same if you are married. Let God lead, don't try to push your spouse in the flesh. Let God work on you and through you. As you start to walk in the way of our Lord Jesus, carrying the fruit of the Holy Spirit, God will take care of the rest. Don't try to rush God's timing, it is truly perfect!

"To one who conquers I will give some
of the hidden manna,
and I will give him a white stone,
with a new name written on the stone
that no one knows except the one who receives it."

(Revelation 2:17 ESV)

Chapter 9

Resurrection, New Name, New Spirit.

Keeping His promise to me, this was the year I was set completely free of all bondage. This came with a sacrifice not understood by many. I didn't even understand the full extent of what it would do. I just knew He was calling me to leave my old life completely behind, slam shut every door, and do it for Him. I chose to walk into the new even though I had nothing but a few bags of clothes. I left people, family, friends, the house, and all my belongings behind.

My daughters were also part of this leaving. They were being oppressed by many spirits at the time. I knew He wanted me to help them and teach them what He taught me about how to fight and bind demons, spirits, and demonic attacks with prayer and the authority we get by speaking the name of Jesus Christ. He wanted them baptized by water and His Holy Spirit fire.

I was told to leave Texas. I had a real live Judas in my life. This person was used by the enemy to destroy, but God used this person to complete the plan He had for me and to show me how mighty He really is. Jesus needed to get to the cross to fulfil His destiny, and Judas was the one God used to make it happen. I was under a custody order, and the girls were supposed to go back to their dad for his Christmas with them. I was told by His Holy Spirit, "You're going to keep them." I didn't know what that meant just yet. All I knew was that I was going to listen to Him no matter what. His ways are higher than our ways. I had an attorney that was also a friend that was helping me through this entire situation. She filed on my behalf and gave me legal advice on what to do. However, God kept pressing, I had to keep the girls.

A few weeks before this Judas moment, I was being warned in dreams about what this person was doing behind my back. God sent someone to confirm it. His Holy Spirit spoke to me, "These people are trying to stop you from moving into the next part of your life, but My daughter, watch Me take them out, remove them, and part the seas for you to cross over. All you have to do is trust and move when I say to move."

The morning He chose for me to leave, it came as a shock to me. I had a dream (nightmare) the night before, I saw this Judas speaking with another person. I knew the person my Judas was talking to. This person paid Judas to end my life. I don't want to go into the details of this tragic dream, but His Spirit spoke to me and said, "My daughter, you must leave today, this dream is literal, but trust Me, if you leave when I tell you to, they won't make it to you. I will ensure they can't."

I was nervous about how this was all going to work. I had many responsibilities I couldn't just leave behind. During my time of packing up (in a hurry) I had two people come to my house with confirmation from the Holy Spirit that I needed to leave. They told me they would stay back and help me with what I had to leave behind, but they felt an urgency for me to leave immediately.

I did not even know where I was going, I was told by His Spirit to get in the car and head towards Virginia. I had never been to Virgina, nor did I know anyone in Virgina. Later that evening as I was on the road, I received two calls. The first one was someone calling me to ask me what was going on, and that the Holy Spirit was putting in their spirit to call me. I told her what God wanted me to do, and where I was supposed to go.

She laughed and said, "Well, now I know why I felt a need to call you. I have a sister, who has a townhome she is not using in Virginia."

I cried as with each step I took in obedience; He sent people to confirm I was on the right path.

The second call came from a friend who said my Judas had both ankles taken out and was bedridden.

I later found out it would be five months before my Judas would be able to walk. I call this person my Judas because they didn't know God was giving me clear insight, revelation and a blueprint how to get around the enemy's traps and snares. I acted like I was clueless when this person kissed me on the cheek before their plan was to go into effect.

I would stop with my girls at restaurants, and people of all ages would come up to me and give me messages from the Holy Spirit. I look back and can clearly see they were His angels. This one older army vet came to me and said, "There are different levels of praying and I see you go to the highest level. God told me to tell you, Isaiah 54:17 to keep going and don't look back."

When we walk closely with God, He will not allow anything to happen to us. He will hold our hand and teach us how to walk around the traps. He cares deeply about every detail in your life.

> *Are you seeing even more why it is so important to have alone time with Him, get to know His voice, and get to know Him?* _____

When I arrived at the townhouse in Virginia, there was no furniture, however, there was a blow-up mattress. I took my girls to get them bedding and pillows and bean bag chairs. We were there four nights. On the fourth night, I knelt and thanked God for all He did. I was grateful we were safe; we were together, and we had a roof over our heads and money in the bank to buy what we needed.

After praying, I heard Him say, "My daughter, go to Cornerstone church tomorrow, the one your friend sent you a sermon from, and sit on the third row, take the girls into the 11 a.m. service with you."

I went and did exactly what He told me. After the service, a woman came to me and told me she felt led to come talk to me. She could tell I was new because the church doesn't recommend parents bringing kids into the main sanctuary.

When she asked me what brought me to the church, I heard the Holy Spirit say, "Tell her you are on an assignment."

After I told her what God said, she wanted to know more, and after we had lunch and spoke, she offered to let us stay at her house.

When you are in His perfect alignment and will for your life, He provides for you the entire way.

I didn't know it at the time, but He had used this person to hide my girls and me until it was the appointed time to be found. One night, after everyone was asleep, He told me the old had come to an end. I could not stop crying as I felt things leave my body. I didn't know what they were, I just felt freer with each passing moment. Bible verses were being poured into my mind. It was overwhelming. I felt like I was floating. After a few hours of feeling this way, His Holy Spirit spoke to me saying He can restore all things and as of that night, my purity and innocence had been restored. I couldn't stop crying because even though it sounded too good to be true, I could feel it. I was different and I didn't know how, but He did it. Through this time, there were many things going on in the background. Many arrows were coming at me. While all who were mocking me were trapped in their overwhelming bondage, He was encompassing me with His love and His freedom!

On May 7, I was walking and praying, and the Holy Spirit said to me, "Amanda, dies tonight. Anyone who is trying to come against you, mock you, do witchcraft, or anything spoken against Amanda won't touch you. As of tonight, you are My re-born warrior and I will no longer speak of the old name, nor will I ever call you the old name again. As of now, you are Natasha Sloane." The definition of the name is: reborn and Christ's birthday. Whereas Sloane, means: warrior.

When I heard this name, I did not recognize it to be a normal name I was used to hearing. I had to go look it up myself. Looking back, He rarely called me by the name Amanda, most of my walk it was "My daughter." I know why now.

The next morning, I was awakened with, "Good morning, My daughter, Natasha, this week is going to be a rough one. You are going to need to mourn Amanda and all her hard work these last years. By the end of the week, I will need you to lay her down at My throne once and for all."

He was right. I was super emotional and in my private time, I would cry. I felt like there was a real death in my life. I was sad and hurt. Toward the end of the week, I was flooded with many visions, but the one I will never forget. I was not only seeing the vision, but I was also taken there. Amanda was at the cross, kneeling, her hands resting on her thighs, and her palms up in complete submission. I saw this very bright woman. She was radiating, I couldn't see her face, but I saw and could feel her love and strength. She walked up to old me, knelt, and said, "It's time." Amanda understood it was time for her to go. The woman hugged Amanda and while this was happening, a huge gold flash and light came over the entire vision. Amanda had somehow disappeared and became one with the woman. The vision zoomed in on the woman. It was me, Natasha. I was in complete shock. The vision kept going, I then saw Natasha, carrying a woman with long black hair in her arms. I saw her arm dangling on the side of Natasha. I couldn't stop crying, I saw it. Natasha was barefoot and carrying Amanda, old me, and was wearing a bright white dress. I, Natasha, walked up to this large throne full of gemstones, jewels that were set in colors which were indescribable. I saw nothing but light coming from the throne, but as I got closer, I saw large feet, and I/ Natasha knelt and placed the old me/Amanda at the throne of Jesus. While I was carrying Amanda, I could feel how tired she was, I could feel her need for rest and it was her time to be at home with the Father.

I heard Him say, "My daughter, Amanda did well and never forget all her hard work, as you could not have been born without Amanda's obedience and fighting to get to this moment."

I was flooded with the verses about new wineskin, Mark 2:22 "and no one puts new wine into old wineskin; or else the new wine bursts the wineskins, the wine is spilled, and the wineskins are ruined. But new wine must be put into new wineskins." A new spirit and a heart of flesh, In Ezekiel 36:26, being reborn again in John 3:3 and many more. This was the night everything I had walked through led to this divine epic moment when I was being made whole and complete in Him.

Many Christians believe the moment they accept Jesus as their personal Lord and savior, they are immediately born again and made new. There is an incorrect understanding the church teaches which is why so many Christians in the church are still stuck in bondage even after years of being a Christian. In Galatians 2:20, Paul writes, "I have been crucified with

Christ, it is no longer I who live, but Christ who lives in me." Paul believed in his heart he was a new creation, but he went away for three years and allowed the Lord Jesus to work with him and help him to be transformed in the image of Christ.

Jesus started all His works and miracles before He was crucified and resurrected. I did not fully become reborn until I/Amanda had many years of having to look at herself and allow Jesus to show her all the areas, she needed uprooted. Something only, He could do. I had to be tested and approved.

"Jesus is the way, the truth, and the life, if you aren't willing to face the truth, you are not willing to face Jesus." If we are not able to face Jesus and the truth the Holy Spirit will bring, then we miss out on the incredible transformation Paul speaks about in the Bible. We miss out on the opportunity to truly be crucified in Christ and to live out a life walking in faith.

Many Christians say all you do is have faith, yet faith does not come from us. Only the Holy Spirit can help us to have faith. The church also teaches we have free will, yet we live in a fallen world of sin where our flesh fights our spirit. If we chose on our own, free will would be to do what we want. Ephesians 2:8-9 says, "For by grace you have been saved through faith. And this is not your own doing; it is the gift of God, not a result of works, so that no one may boast." In 1 John 4:6, it says, "We are from God. Whoever knows

God listens to us; whoever is not from God does not listen to us."

Churches have given a false sense of security. This is why people are stuck. They are stuck in sin, they are stuck with spirits, demonic attacks, addictions, unhealthy cycles and failing mindsets. They are stuck with going to church on Sunday and not seeing any difference in them or their lives.

When someone is crucified in Christ and resurrected, they literally change from the inside out. Galatians 2:20-21 says, "It is not me who lives, but Christ who lives in me."

Repenting, and asking Jesus to come into your life is not the last step, it is the very first step in becoming crucified in Christ and resurrected in Him; what the church calls a re-born Christian. Nowhere in the Bible does it talk about a sinner's prayer. It says in *Romans 10:9 "because, if you confess with your mouth Jesus is Lord and believe in your heart that God raised him from the dead, you will be saved."* Many people speak it with their mouth, but they don't know how to believe in their heart and walk it out in their actions. They need the Holy Spirit to help them.

Ask Yourself...

> *Have I accepted Jesus into my heart, but still have the same anger problems?*

How about, the same need to be validated by worldly things?

Do I still feel depressed, fearful, worried, and anxious?

Am I still carrying the same baggage as when I accepted Christ into my heart?

Since going to a church do I feel there is even more bondage then when I started?

Do I still have the same habits I had when I accepted Christ in my heart?

If the answer is *yes* to any of these questions, then you are still in the very first steps over becoming crucified and resurrected in Christ and your journey is just getting started.

I am excited for you. This is not something to be upset about or feel less about, this means you are on your way to freedom. The previous chapters are your guide on how to grow your relationship with God and how to walk out a life in surrender and obedience that leads to a life being set free in Christ.

God is always examining and testing things in your heart. David said, "Search my heart O' God, and remove anything that offends you." I have to ask for forgiveness multiple times a day. Many times in the past, even if a thought comes into my mind, I have to do what Paul says and, "take every thought captive and bring it under the obedience of God."

Later, my mom she told me she felt I had died, and she was never going to see me again. She constantly says how my entire character, demeanor, and personality changed. We looked back at photos, and realized my physical facial features looked different and brighter. Not to mention, my chronic back pain was gone, my anemia went away, and many other issues I had with health went away overnight. Some of you may be asking, when you are fully reborn in Christ, is your name going to be changed. I can't answer that for you. What I can tell you is my name had to be changed, and for a short while, I didn't fully understand why until after talking with my mom.

Seven months after Natasha laid Amanda at the throne of Jesus, in my alone time with the Lord, His Spirit said there were many reasons why He changed my name. One of the most pressing ones was that my name placed a curse over me to cause a premature death over my life. When He told me to legally change my name, I let my mom know. My mom accepted my name, but had a hard time calling me another name. She gave me the name she loved, and thought was perfect for me. I thought the name was beautiful too.

The Holy Spirit soon revealed to mom and me during one of our conversations that the name she gave me was cursed because she chose the name from someone she admired in high school, but sadly died in a car accident at the age of seventeen. When I was seventeen, I had an extremely bad car accident. The Lord told me I was supposed to die that day, but He protected me.

I am sure your body is in chills as you read this. I walked around my whole life with a curse. The enemy kept sending people to fulfill that curse of premature death and destruction over my life. We both cried and thanked the Holy Spirit for revealing the why to us. I thanked Him for my new name, but more so my name came with no curses and no bondage. I literally was completely and irrevocably free. A promise He made to me in 2017 had finally come to pass.

Months before I was able to talk to my mom about my name, there was one special night His Holy Spirit opened the Heavens, and I was ushered into the spirit realm. I saw this warrior looking person with armor so bright and on fire. This warrior was getting ready. When she took her helmet off and bowed to the throne of Jesus Christ, it was me. I saw angels come to me, and touch my mouth, my ears, my hands, my head, my eyes, my throat, my feet, and my stomach.

I heard His mighty voice say, "My daughter, I speak Jeremiah 1 over your life. In the past, you prophesied, but now you will prophesy louder than ever before, and as of tonight, you are ready to know you are My prophet. There is a rarity to you I will reveal later. You are a prophet to the nations. You have known this in your spirit, and many people have come in the past to tell you, you were one. But it wasn't time for me to speak this to you. Now is your time. I can trust you. My daughter, know this, you obey Me through and through, and you won't fail."

His Holy Spirit went on to tell me that my prayers led by His Holy Spirit could activate things to shift into alignment and when He sent someone in my life, I was there to help them be activated and launched into their calling. Again, He was the one doing this through me. He gets all the glory.

The same night, He took me deeper into what He put me here on earth to accomplish in Him. "I have to make you extremely relatable" He said. I was about to enter the greatest experience I would have in my life, one that softened my heart and opened my eyes to God's true power.

The Dreams

God was showing me what was about to come; I had two dreams. The first one, I saw myself in a prison. I jumped from the top of the dream, and I had a sword, it was on fire. I took the sword and was able to slice through the steel doors. The prisoners were grey, dark, and tired. I took their hands, touched their hearts, gave them a Bible which turned in to a sword. They lit up in color and ran out with their swords to fight.

The second dream, I saw a man with a blurred face, my girls, and me in a truck on the beach. We were driving and my nails and my toes were painted bright orange. I saw the word freedom all over the dream. I could feel my freedom, peace, and love. I felt and saw joy on my face. I knew in my spirit I was about to be taken to jail. I knew He was sending me and even though it was scary to realize or admit it, I knew I was ready.

I praised Him for the time I was given. Even though I knew there were going to be days I wouldn't know what to do I knew He was going to be with me. So, I made the best of my last days with my girls. We had so much fun. I made sure we prayed harder, talked more about what God's plans were, and how we had to keep praying and trusting Him. I asked God to draw my girls to Him and that they would know Him the way I do, and to take them deeper, but at a young age. The biggest prayer we prayed was for their father to be saved and for God to wake him up from the spiritual coma he was in. It was time for him to die and be brought to life in Christ.

My prayer was about to be answered, and God was going to use me as an instrument. What would look like suffering was really Him sending me to complete the work He started in me and in redeeming all that had been lost.

"Creation itself will be set free from its bondage to corruption and obtain the freedom of the glory of the children of God."

(Romans 8:21 ESV)

Chapter 10

Freedom in Captivity

There will be people in your life that may not even be bad, but God has to remove them anyway. There are some who do not wish you good, but the ones who have no ill will towards you sometimes still can't go where God is taking you. He must remove those who cannot partake in your blessing because their time in your life is over. There are many times we try to keep people we want, but in the end, whether we accept it or not, God will have His way and He will remove them when it is time. He will allow events to occur that will cause them to fear, misunderstand, or even harden their hearts toward you to ensure they do not partake in the blessings He has for you.

When you walk in complete obedience, some will misunderstand you, get confused with how you talk in faith, and how you speak with a different kind of wisdom. Some will even attack you and say you are lying or doing witchcraft. The enemy is trying to get you to doubt and cause you to stumble so you won't make it to the gates of your calling and destiny. Right before the debut of Natasha, I needed to be tested. All that was attached to Amanda's life had to die. Every door had to be slammed shut.

Obedience doesn't always come with the details one would expect.

There were tests that came with carrying the mantle He gave me. They led to my arrest for following the Lord. I had to be still and listen as I was handcuffed. If I didn't have the Holy Spirit telling me I was right where He wanted me, I would have felt lost. He kept reminding me how the Apostle Paul died to himself every day. He obeyed God with each step he took, and he still ended up in prison.

Pause and Reflect...

Take a few minutes to read Acts 16:16-34.

Why were Paul and Silas arrested?

_____

_____

What did they do in spite of the horrible conditions in the prison?

_____

_____

What happened because of their obedience to God?

_____

_____

God went on to speak to me while I was being arrested. He said He was exposing the hearts of so-called friends. He told me they would all turn on me because they were not allowed to go where He was taking me. He said He was preserving and hiding me until the appointed time.

As I was placed in the backseat of the police car, God continued explaining I had much work to do in jail and I was placed on assignment in a place where some of His strongest soldiers have been placed. Even though everyone mocked me, plastered my arrest report all over social media, and twisted everything around, it didn't matter. God wanted them to write Amanda off for good. People I thought were my friends let fear and the flesh get in the way, but God knew what He was doing. I was walking in complete freedom, so even in a place of captivity, I was free!

The Lord did so many things for me while I was in jail in Maryland. Upon meeting the inmates, they were all very welcoming and could tell it was my first time to ever be in jail. The first night, we all gathered together, and they allowed me to pray for each one of their charges. Everyone helped me understand how certain things were done in jail. God really does work out every detail of your life. A detail I knew was all Him, was the computer "accidently" condensed my photo changing the look of my face to where I didn't even recognize the picture to be me. Then, He used an old last name, not my current last name so anyone who looked me up would not have been able to find me under the last name many knew me by.

His Spirit made me a promise, "I will never let you look foolish."

The day I was being extradited; the agent lost her bag. Inside, it contained the jacket where the hand-cuffs were supposed to be strapped to. The agent and I chatted the whole way to the airport, and by the time we got there, God had spoken to her through me. It did not look in any way like I was an inmate being transferred. I had shorts on and a t-shirt. The agent let me walk with her like a friend, and she got me break-fast and coffee. We sat on the plane as if we were trav-eling as friends laughing and talking. God again spoke through me to her throughout the entire flight, about personal things which included her wanting to end her life. When we landed in Houston, she got us a nice rental. She parked it for a few hours while we spoke and at the end, I prayed over her and with her. We are still friends today.

I was transferred to Harris County Jail where I had to be placed in a cell for Covid. I could only come out of the cell for one hour and spend the other 23 hours in the cell. I didn't have anything. I prayed and cried to the Lord, "I trust You. I know I heard You right. If I could ask for anything, it would be to have Your Word. That's all I want."

I asked around when people would be removed from their cells to have their hour out. No one could find one and no one could get me one. Where I was placed, I could hear cell doors open and close, everything echoed.

I was sitting with the Lord in my cell, when I heard a male voice speak, "Heard you needed a Bible."

Then, I saw a blue and gold Bible slide under my door. I ran to peek out my window, but there was no one. There was no sound of any door opening, and no sound of anyone coming or going. I grabbed the Bible and hugged it tight. I heard His Spirit say, "I sent him to you."

I was extremely blessed, as many people had been in their cells for weeks, and I was blessed with only being in there for seven days. On the sixth day, I placed the Bible on the filthy floor next to a drawing of a cross another inmate made for me, along with orange peels and soap. I said this is all I have to give you dad. I got on my knees and prayed. I thanked Him and said if this was the cup He had for me, I was going to accept it. I loved Him so much, my life was not my own, it was His. I was going to serve Him no matter what happened.

Even though I looked like I was in captivity, I was free. I prayed my heart out, but I wasn't asking for my release. I asked Him to use me. I asked for spiritual wisdom, to see more, and for Him to take me deeper. I wasn't asking to get out, I just wanted what He wanted for me. He spoke so much to me that night, but I want to keep it between Him and me. One thing He did say was that starting the next day, my life was going to change for the better.

The next day, I woke up and heard I was being transferred. While I was in my cell giving Him thanks for the cup He had given me, He was rearranging my housing for the next four months. I was transferred to the top trustee tank in the jail. It was then God confirmed I was not taken to jail; He had sent me.

After talking with a fellow sister in Christ who had spent her life in and out of prison, she became very excited when she found out my charge. She brought me a verse when He told her, "Natasha is the fugitive I promised you was coming." Ezekiel 24:26 says, "On that day a fugitive will come to you to report to you the news." She then went on to tell me she had been waiting for the fugitive. The Lord told her someone was coming (she would have been charged with being a fugitive) and when that happened, she would know

He was Lord, and she was going to make it. The fugitive would bring good news. She thought it was going to be when she was transferred back to the county her case was in. She was surprised it was in this county. The Lord spoke to her through me about a family matter, and that it was going to work out. Not too long after, she reported back to me the news of this family member, and the praise reports.

They knew the name on my wrist band said Amanda, but everyone knew me as Natasha. When they asked, I told them my story. God gave me so much favor in jail. There were a few times when opposition came against me, however not long after holding His hand through it they were either removed, went home, or transferred. He made way for an enjoyable experience all around. There were times inmates and even detention officers asked me if I was undercover. Through my time as a trustee, I met some incredible people, and I got to pray with everyone before court. I led bible studies and loved on everyone who came in. Even in the opposition, nothing got to a point of feeling like I was not where I was supposed to be.

There were two women in particular that stood out as gifts from God, they made my experience much more insightful. God used these young women in many ways and made me a better Natasha. Meeting them showed me inmates are not their charges and gave me such compassion for inmates all over. The inmates helped me to develop great leadership skills. I saw firsthand God can bring the most beautiful people in our lives in the most unexpected places.

The Lord challenged me. I was Natasha, but Amanda's name was on my wrist. I was free, yet with Amanda's charge of "interference with child custody." Every morning, His Holy Spirit would tell me, "You are who I say you are." The greatest lesson of all came towards the end of my stay at Harris County Jail. I knew I would not leave that place until I conquered the one enemy who had been trying to destroy everything for years. The one who had tried to control me, situations in my life, my husband and later my children. All at the forefront of trying to ensure my girls would not have me as their mother. The one who had been trying to set me up to look bad, trying to break me, but it only did the opposite. I won't speak of who this is, out of respect for the Holy Spirit. I only want Him to be glorified in this book.

His Holy Spirit renewed my way of thinking and gave me a complete paradigm shift. He told me, "My daughter, I sent this person in your life, though you may think you found this person, but I am the one who ordained your days.

I have used this person to go against you, which caused you not only to surrender to Me, but you also allowed me to transform you and now you are a new creation in Me. I hand selected this enemy just for you, and their time of trying to come against you ended when you left Texas and became Natasha."

"This person was your Old Testament Saul who was the one I used to help push David into his destiny. I used this person to teach you how-to walk-through fire and to show you how to ask Me to walk with you. I used her to develop and make a warrior out of you. My daughter, she was My gift to you. You can't be angry with her, I want you to forgive her, and thank Me for giving her to you."

He took me to Romans 9:20-23. "But who are you, O man to answer back to God? Will that be molded say to its molder, 'why have you made me like this?' Has the potter no right over the clay, to make out of the same lump one vessel for honorable use and another for dishonorable use…"

He said, "My daughter, praise Me, this person did what they were meant to do in your life, and they are gone now never to return."

Another example from the scriptures is the story of Joseph who was sold into slavery by his brothers. Read what Joseph said to his brothers Genesis 45:5.

"I am the one you sold into Egypt, but don't be upset. And don't be angry with yourselves because you sold me here. God sent me ahead of you to save many lives….He sent me here to save your lives by an act of mighty power."

How has this helped you understand why you have had to face some difficult situations even from family or friends?

Our enemies are sometimes given to us as part of God's plan to get us where He wants us to be. When my enemies thought they could get everyone to assassinate my character and would be able to boast about me going to jail, it was really God's plan all along to spread the gospel, and to bring glory to His mighty name. Our enemies are instruments God uses to make us better.

Pause and Ask Yourself...

Is there an enemy in my life, or perhaps a few?

Do I know who they are?

Can I see how God has been using them in my life?

How does understanding that my enemy was hand selected by God help me to handle the situation moving forward?

What insight has God given me in Romans 9:23?

_____

_____

One of the things God said to me when I first started this journey was it would be long and brutal, but it had to be. He made me a promise, though.

He said, "My daughter, your journey has to be long and painful, so you can learn step-by-step with Me. In the future I will have you teach and guide others, so their storms can be shortened and they can learn how to have an intimate relationship with Me. Your pain and journey will not be in vain, and many people will not have to go through the same mistakes. They will know I AM still the same God and I never change. I want my children to have a relationship with Me. Carry your mantle with honor and keep your head up. You are Mine and I am with you."

Pray and thank your heavenly Father right now for how He is leading you to where you can receive His full blessing and your children can reap a powerful legacy as well.

> *"Or do you not know that your body is a temple of the Holy Spirit within you, whom you have from God? You are not your own, for you were bought with a price. So*

glorify God in your body." (1 Corinthians 6:19-21 ESV)

Maintaining freedom in Him.

People have asked me, "can we really maintain freedom in the land of the living?" The answer is yes. I explain to them, when we are whole and free in Jesus Christ that doesn't mean we won't fall short of His glory. It doesn't mean we won't get attacked spiritually, nor does it mean we stop growing in Him. What it means is that we no longer desire worldly things. We desire to live a holy life, walking the path of and pursuing righteousness. We live to bring glory and honor to our King.

We live with a heart posture consistently willing to repent and accept when we are wrong. We desire meekness, humility and all the fruits of the Holy Spirit. We do not want to dishonor His holiness or sovereignty. We never stop having a reverent fear of who He is. We walk in His rest and peace. We have accepted He is the one who wrote out our days and all we need to do is fix our eyes on Jesus and trust He holds us in the palm of His hand. We truly walk a life not only believing but knowing that we may be in this world but we are not of it. We no longer pursue worldly things and possessions. We know He is the treasure, our reward and our prize. Nothing in this world can give us what He can.

We fix our eyes on what is true, pure, lovely, of good report, what is of virtue, what is praiseworthy and what is just. We fix our eyes on what is holy and what brings Jesus Christ glory. We no longer live for ourselves, but we accept the cup He gave us and we give ourselves over to Him completely to do what He wants us to accomplish for His glory. Through the storm and the tests, we still praise Him because we know He is doing a new work in us. We die to our flesh daily and we crave obedience. We wake up asking Him how we can serve Him. He already died on the cross for us, that is more than enough. Lastly, we walk knowing we will be hated by the world, and we find joy in that fact because we are hated for Jesus and that is better than anything this world has to offer. We become a living testimony of the wonderous miracle working God we serve and love.

This world is fading and what we do here on earth matters. We must fix our hearts on eternity. We must take people's salvation seriously and we must stop making it about what we want. Many people have experienced miracles, healing and deliverance. God loves to show His people He is alive. I believe one of the greatest miracles we can truly ever experience in life is the miracle of being reborn in Jesus Christ and that He transforms you from the inside out to reflect Him.

Heavenly Father, Jesus Christ and the Holy Spirit, the great I AM is always speaking. The question is are you willing to listen? I hear Him saying "*I AM your Abba, I AM He, you can stop searching for what will only leave you empty. Run to Me and I will set you free. It won't always be easy, but nothing compares to the joy and the reward coming! I WANT you for eternity!*"

Conclusion

Final Word

I pray my walk with our Father, His Holy Spirit, and Jesus has enlightened you and has brought you some tools and weapons to put to use in your own journey and relationship with Him.

The Bible is a map, a handbook, a guide, and a love letter showing us how to take back what God gave us. He wants us to be free in this life. He created earth for humans to enjoy and be free. Adam and Eve ate from the tree that brought death, but God brought Jesus to bring redemption. The Bible is to show us how to achieve redemption for what was done in the past and for us to live under God's grace which brings us the ultimate freedom.

He does not want us to be trapped. Even though sometimes things can sound good, there is no easy way to get to freedom. Just like Jesus had to suffer and learn through His obedience. He was sent here to give His life for our Father's purpose. We too must endure and face the same things. We too must surrender to His will for our life, pick up our cross, be crucified, and be re-born. When we do, we truly can walk in His rest and freedom here on earth. Then we can go to our home in heaven and be eternally free.

Our Father wants to meet you where you're at, take your hand, walk you through to the truth, help you to face what you need to face, and show you how not to waste even one single day in bondage.

When you picked up this book, it was your divine appointment. HE started speaking to you through the pages. He is letting you know it is your appointed hour and you are right on time. Remember, you are already fighting from the victory of Jesus Christ! It's time to take your place in His Kingdom and be reborn in Him.

Brothers and Sisters, I have one last question for you to answer:

Are you ready to be Forged in His Fire?

_____

_____

Who the Son sets free is free indeed. (John 8:36)

Where the Spirit of the Lord is there is liberty. (2 Corinthians 3:17)

Father, this book was from You, not me.

I was the vessel that brought forth some of Your heavenly keys.

May You water these seeds,

May they each grow and reap

A bountiful harvest to bring You glory.

Father may each one who reads this book know You are for them.

May they know it's their appointed time and how You love them.

You are the only one who can right every wrong for them.

You take what the enemy meant for evil, and You use it for good.

These precious children of Yours have been misunderstood,

Please take their hand and walk with them

All the way to the truth.

I love you all,
– Natasha

> *"I have been crucified with Christ; It is no*
> *longer I who lives, but Christ lives in me."*
> (Galatians 2:20)

Epilogue

The Great Commission

Family, this book was not just written for your enter-tainment. While I hope you enjoyed my journey so far with the Lord, this was much more than a story and or a testimony. It was written as a guide in how to have a per-sonal and intimate relationship with our Father, Jesus Christ, and His Holy Spirit. It is a call to action on your part. One of the major takeaways I want you to see, is that in order to walk in freedom and allow Him to forge you in His fire, you will need consistency. God is looking for an end time army that will step up and fight the good fight, not only by teaching the gospel, but by being the gospel. In order to stand strong in the Lord and to be equipped ready to fight, you will need fortitude, disci-pline, endurance, determination, and the mindset that you must not give up, no matter how hard it gets. Life does not get easier, you only become stronger.

The closer we get to the Lord, Jesus Christ, and His Holy Spirit, the stronger we will become. We have the authority through our savior and battle commander Jesus Christ to drive the enemy out of our life. Jesus already conquered the enemy and disarmed all the rulers, principalities, and dark spiritual forces when He was crucified and resurrected. Lester Sumrall said it best, "We don't talk the devil out of our life or someone, we drive and cast him out."

This book is a guide to start to put the "watered down Christianity" away and pick up the meat of the gospel. When God clothed Gideon with His Holy Spirit, he clothed him with His power. The power of the Holy Spirit is available to anyone who is willing to give their life and submit their will under the Lordship of Jesus Christ.

Let's pick up the sword of the Spirit, armor up, and get to work. We are needed to not only become equipped in the Lord, but also called to equip others.

If this book impacted your life during your read or after, please share your testimony with us either through email at: FIHFMinistries@mail.com, message me on Instagram @ForgedinHisfire24 or you can share it on all social media platforms, hashtag #forgedinhisfiretestimony. My hope and desire is for Forged in His Fire to remain interactive.

About the Author

Natasha is a writer and has a ministry called "Forged in His Fire Ministries." She enjoys hiking, reading, and writing when she is not with her family. She is the mother of two precious daughters, who inspired her to pick up her cross and walk out an obedient life.

Printed in the USA
CPSIA information can be obtained
at www.ICGtesting.com
LVHW051629280524
781186LV00017B/359